Medals of America

presents

United States Military Medals
1939 to Present

By

Lawrence H. Borts
and
Col. (Ret.) Frank C. Foster

3rd Edition

> *Dedicated to America's finest citizens; her*
> *veterans and active military with the*
> *families who support them . . .*
> *God Bless You All!*

Hardcover Edition ISBN — 1-884452-12-4
Softcover Edition ISBN — 1-884452-13-2

Library of Congress
Catalog Card Number — 93-80445

Published by:
MOA Press (Medals of America Press)
1929 Fairview Road, Fountain Inn, S.C.
29644-9137
(803) 862-6051

Printed in the United States of America
by Keys Printing Co.
Greenville, South Carolina

ABOUT THE AUTHORS

LONNY BORTS

FRANK FOSTER

Lawrence "Lonny" Borts developed a lifelong interest in military awards as a boy in New York City during World War II. After graduating from the New York University College of Engineering, he spent most of his professional life with the Grumman Corporation, retiring in 1992 as an Engineering Specialist. He maintains one of the largest collections of military ribbons in the world and is consultant to a number of the U. S. Armed Forces directorates and medals research societies. He is also the Awards Program Director of Vanguard, Inc., the largest supplier of military uniform equipment in the U. S. and realized every enthusiast's dream when he co-designed the Coast Guard "E" Ribbon. He and Beverly, his bride of nearly 40 years now reside in Melbourne, Florida.

Col. Frank C. Foster (USA , Ret'd), graduated from the Citadel in 1964 and saw service as a Battery Commander in Germany and in Vietnam with the 173rd Airborne Brigade. In the Adjutant General's Corps, he served as the Adjutant General of the Central Army Group, the 4th Infantry Division and was the Commandant and Chief of the Army's Adjutant General's Corps from 1986 to 1990. His military service provided him a unique view of the Armed Forces Awards System. He currently operates Medals of America Press. He and his wife Linda, who was decorated with the Army Commander's Medal in 1990, for service to the Army, live in Fountain Inn, South Carolina.

GRATEFUL ACKNOWLEDGEMENTS

The authors wish to express their deepest appreciation to the following individuals for their invaluable contributions. Without their unselfish efforts, this book would have ended as an unfulfilled dream.

Richard Bush for color plates. Mr. Bush makes fine art prints and custom enlarging. He studied photography under Jerry Ulesmann at the University of Florida.

The entire Medals of America team with special thanks to: Mrs. Lois Owens for custom mounting, Mrs. Linda Foster, Major Bill Foss, USAR (relentless proof reading), LTC (Ret.) Tony Aldebol for suggestions.

COL. (Ret.) Gerald T. Luchino, Mr. Thomas B. Proffitt and Mr. Robert L. Hopkins of The Institute of Heraldry, U.S. Army.

COL. (Ret.) F. P. Anthony and Mrs. Rose of the U.S. Marine Corps Military Awards Branch, Human Resources Division.

Ms. Shelby (Jeanne) Kirk, currently serving as Head of the U.S. Navy Awards and Special Projects Branch.

Ms. Dianne E. Porter, currently serving as U.S. Coast Guard Military Personnel Management Specialist. Ms. Porter is also the individual who gave Col. Foster's telephone number to Mr. Borts and started the dream.

Mr. Lee Graves, Air Force veteran and President of GRACO Industries, one of the leading medal manufacturers in the United States.

Mrs. White and her fine team at the U. S. Army Awards Branch.

CMSgt. Steve Haskin, Ribbon Bank Manager of the Orders and Medals Society of America.

Mr. Bill Gershen, President and CEO of Vanguard, Inc.

Ms. Patricia A. Thomas, Office of Maritime Labor & Training, Maritime Administration, Department of Transportation.

LT(jg) Jim Mathieu, U. S. Coast Guard Defense Operations Division.

Mr. Ben Keys and Ms. Rita Handler of Keys Printing in Greenville, SC, for their dedication to this book.

TABLE OF CONTENTS

LIST OF ILLUSTRATIONS

1. INTRODUCTION TO THE 3RD EDITION

One evening, just as I was wrapping up my day's activities at Medals of America, I received a telephone call which started off: "Why haven't I heard of you before?" The caller introduced himself as a Mr. Lonny Borts and, when I said I have never heard of **him** either, we both laughed. While the world of military medals is small, it is specialized. The obvious answer is that Medals of America, focuses on veterans awards, rather than collectors and researchers, so there was little likelihood that we would cross paths in spite of our mutual membership in several organizations.

When Lonny described some of his work in the decorations and awards field, my level of excitement rose and I asked for a copy. Reading the material, I realized that Lonny is one of the foremost experts in the U.S. military awards field. I was so impressed by the level of detail and completeness of his efforts that I immediately proposed a book to cover the entire spectrum of U. S. Military awards since World War II.

The collaborative effort from that initial exchange of ideas culminated in the first edition of this book. This book is designed to be a definitive reference covering United States decorations, medals and ribbons for veterans and active duty personnel. It is also designed to be a single source for the military decorations and medals of each service. Most of the material was derived from the latest military awards and uniform manuals and other authoritative sources, although the authors' personal opinions may have slipped in from time to time.

When the first edition was conceived, the perils of producing an absolutely up-to-date, definitive reference on any subject were fully recognized. This was especially true in the dynamic world of U.S. military awards which, up to that time, had produced 75 awards in 47 years, an average of 1.5 new awards per year since the unification of the Armed Forces in 1947.

Almost as predictable as the tides, since this book's original publication date, the U.S. military has issued three new awards. The Department of Defense has also accepted the Kuwaiti Medal for the Liberation of Kuwait, thus increasing the number of awards created since 1947 to 78. Just as important, the number of updated regulations that were issued by the U.S. military since the original printing virtually ordained that another edition, containing the very latest information, be made available to veterans, military personnel, collectors and enthusiasts everywhere.

Owing to the complimentary reviews enjoyed by the first and second editions, the original format (text and illustrations on facing pages) is retained while the contents are updated to reflect the current state of U.S. awards and decorations. In addition, most pages have been revamped to improve readability and a new section on medal clasps/bars has been added to enhance the reader's comprehension of this very complex subject. Finally, in what has become a trade mark, we are pleased to present the graphic debut of three new awards, never before seen in any reference: the Armed Forces Service Medal, the Transportation Distinguished Service Medal, and the Emirate of Kuwait's Liberation of Kuwait Medal.

And then there's that ugly word; **MISTEAKS**. Every book in print, probably dating back to the Gutenberg Bible, no matter how high-sounding, brilliantly conceived or well-intentioned, is bound to possess its share of factual errors and mispelled words. A few errors were discovered in the first edition and appropriate corrections made in the text and graphical presentations. If any further errors are detected, please accept our apologies, drop us a line and be assured that they will be corrected in future editions. In this spirit, we will start the ball rolling by pointing out that the words "MISTEAKS" and "mispelled" in the first sentence of this paragraph are both misspelled.

It is hoped that the third edition will provide you with the same insights and informational value as the first two editions. We look forward to help from our readers to improve future editions.

Col.(Ret.) Frank C. Foster   Lonny Borts
Fountain Inn, SC   Melbourne, FL

August, 1995

BACKGROUND OF UNITED STATES AWARDS

The Andre Medal awarded to patriots Van Wert, Paulding and Williams by Continental Congress in 1780.

AMERICAN REVOLUTION — The chronicle of military decorations in the United States begins early in the American Revolution, when Congress voted to award gold medals to outstanding military leaders. The first such medal was struck to honor George Washington for his service in driving the British from Boston in 1776. Similar medals were bestowed upon General Horatio Gates for his victory at the Battle of Saratoga and Captain John Paul Jones after his famous naval engagement with the Serapis in 1779. Unlike present practice, however, these were large, presentation medals not designed to be worn on the military uniform. Interestingly, once the dies were cut, many copies were manufactured and distributed as commemorative medals to instill patriotic pride in the new country's victories. As a matter of interest, many of these early commemorative medallions are still being struck and offered for sale by the U. S. Mint.

The "Andre" medal broke the custom of restricting the award of medals to successful senior officers and is doubly unique in that it was designed for wear around the neck. The medal was presented by Congress in 1780 to the three enlisted men who captured Major John Andre with the plans of the West Point fortifications in his boot.

In August, 1782, George Washington established the Badge of Military Merit, the first U. S. decoration which had general application to all enlisted men, and one which he hoped would inaugurate a permanent awards system. At the same time, he expressed his fundamental awards philosophy when he issued an order from his headquarters at Newburgh, New York, which read:

"The General, ever desirous to cherish a virtuous ambition in his soldiers, as well as to foster and encourage every species of military merit, directs that, whenever any singularly meritorious action is performed, the author of it shall be permitted to wear on his facings, over his left breast, the figure of a heart in purple cloth or silk, edged with narrow lace or binding. Not only instances of unusual gallantry, but also of extraordinary fidelity, and essential service in any way, shall meet with a due reward...the road to glory in a patriot army and a free country is thus opened to all. This order is also to have retrospect to the earliest days of the war, and to be considered a permanent one."

Although special and commemorative medals had been awarded previously, until this point no decoration had been established which honored the private soldier with a reward for special merit. The wording of the order is worth careful study. The object was "to cherish a virtuous ambition" and to "to foster and encourage every species of military merit." Note also, that Washington appreciated that every kind of service was important by proposing to reward, "not only instances of unusual gallantry, but also of extraordinary fidelity and essential service in any way." And finally, the wonderfully democratic sentence, "the road to glory in a patriotic army and free country is thus opened to all."

Coming as it did, almost a year after Cornwallis' surrender at Yorktown, the message was never given widespread distribution and, as a result, there were only three known recipients of this badge, Sergeants Elijah Churchill, William Brown and Daniel Bissell. Unfortunately, after the Revolution, the award fell into disuse and disappeared for 150 years.

However, it did not die, primarily due to the efforts of the Army's then Chief of Staff, General Douglas MacArthur, (and, by no accident, one of its first recipients). On the 200th anniversary of Washington's birth, February 22, 1932, the War Department announced that:

"By order of the President of the United States, the Purple Heart, established by Gen. George Washington at Newburgh, New York . . . is hereby revived out of respect to his memory and military achievements."

1782 Badge of Military Merit and 1932 Purple Heart.

Washington's "figure of a heart in purple" was retained as the medal's central theme and embellished with Washington's likeness and his coat of arms. The words "For Military Merit" appear on the reverse as a respectful reference to its worthy predecessor.

CIVIL WAR - In the eighty years after the Revolution, the United States engaged in at least two major conflicts with foreign nations (War of 1812, War with Mexico), but no attempt was made to revive or reestablish a comprehensive awards program. The Certificate of Merit was established by the Army in 1847 to reward soldiers who distinguished themselves in battle, but this was not translated into medallic form until 1905. In 1861, the Medal of Honor was established for enlisted personnel of the U. S. Navy, followed the next year by the creation of its Army counterpart for NCO's and private soldiers. Officers were made eligible for the award in later years.

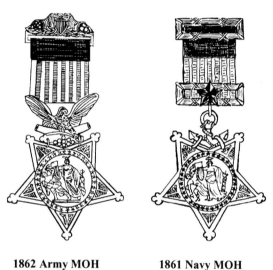

1862 Army MOH   1861 Navy MOH

SPANISH AMERICAN WAR — For nearly twenty years, the Medal of Honor remained the sole American military award of any kind. Although the Navy and Marine Corps had authorized the first Good Conduct Medals in the 1880's, it was not until the eve of the 20th Century that a host of medals were authorized to commemorate the events surrounding the Spanish-American War. This was future President Theodore Roosevelt's "Bully Little War" that produced <u>seven</u> distinct medals for only four months of military action.

The first of these was the medal to commemorate the victory of the naval forces under the command of Commodore Dewey over the Spanish fleet at Manila Bay. This award was notable as it was the first such medal in U. S. history to be awarded to all officers and enlisted personnel present during a specific military expedition.

When Roosevelt, an ardent supporter of the military, ultimately reached the White House, he took it upon himself to legislate for the creation of medals to honor all those who had served in America's previous conflicts. Thus, by 1908, the U.S. had authorized campaign medals, some retroactive, for the Civil War, Indian Wars, War with Spain, Philippine Insurrection and China relief Expedition of 1900-01. While the services used the same ribbons, different medals were struck. Also, the custom of wearing service ribbons on the tunic was adopted during this same time frame (using different precedences). Thus, the Services managed to establish the principle of independence in the creation and wearing of awards that is virtually unchanged today.

WORLD WAR I — At the time of the U. S. entry into World War I, the Medal of Honor, Certificate of Merit and Navy/Marine Good Conduct Medal still represented America's entire inventory of personal decorations. This presented the twin dangers that the Medal of Honor might be cheapened by being awarded too often and that other deeds of valor might go unrecognized. By 1918, popular agitation forced the authorization of two new awards, the Army's Distinguished Service Cross and Distinguished Service Medal, created by Executive Order in 1918. In the same year, the traditional U. S. refusal to permit the armed forces to accept foreign decorations was rescinded, allowing military personnel to accept awards from the grateful Allied governments. In 1919, the Navy created the Navy Cross and its own Distinguished Service Medal for Navy and Marine Corps personnel.

**Army Distinguished   Navy Cross
Service Cross**

The issuance of the World War I Victory medal established another precedent, that of wearing clasps with the names of individual battles on the suspension ribbon of a campaign medal. This was an ongoing practice in many countries, most notably Britain and France, since the 19th Century. When the ribbon bar alone was worn, each clasp was represented by a small (3/16" diameter) bronze star. Fourteen such clasps were adopted along with five clasps to denote service in specific countries. However, the latter were issued

World War I Victory Medal with Ribbon Bars

only if no battle clasp was earned. Only one service clasp could be issued to any individual and they were not represented by a small (3/16") bronze star on the ribbon bar.

It is a final irony that the British, who were the greatest proponents of the practice, never issued a single bar with their own version of the Victory Medal.

During this same period, the Army used a 3/16" diameter silver star to indicate a citation for gallantry during any previous campaign, dating back to the Civil War. An officer or enlisted man so cited was also presented with a Silver Star citation, which evolved into the Silver Star Medal in 1932.

Between the two World Wars, American troops were dispatched to such areas as Haiti, Nicaragua and China to quell rebellions and deal with civil unrest and appropriate medals were authorized to commemorate these events.

WORLD WAR II — On September 8, 1939, in response to the growing threat of involvement in World War II, the President proclaimed a National Emergency in order to increase the size of the U. S. military forces. For the first time, a peacetime service award, the American Defense Service Medal, was authorized for wear by those personnel who served in the military, prior to the attack on Pearl Harbor on December 7, 1941.

The onset of America's participation in World War II saw a significant increase in both personal decorations and campaign medals. Since U. S. forces were serving **all** over the world, a campaign medal was designed for each major (and carefully defined) area. The three medals for the American, Asiatic-Pacific and European-African-Middle Eastern Campaigns encompassed the globe. However, the World War I practice of using campaign bars was discarded in favor of 3/16" bronze stars that could denote any military endeavor, from a major invasion, to a submarine war patrol.

World War II, introduced the first (and only!) service medal unique to female military personnel. Known as the Women's Army Corps Service Medal, it was authorized for service in both the W.A.C. and its predecessor, the Women's Army Auxiliary

Corps. In addition, the war saw the large scale award of foreign medals and decorations to American servicemen. The Philippine Government, for one, authorized awards to commemorate the Defense and Liberation of their island country. The first foreign award designed strictly for units, the Philippine Presidential Unit Citation, patterned after a similar American award, was also approved for wear by American forces at this time. In the European Theater, France and Belgium made many presentations of their War Crosses (Croix de Guerre) to U. S. military personnel.

The next mid-war period, from 1945 to 1950, saw the introduction of two counterparts of previous World War I awards, the Victory and Occupation Medals. This time, no bars or clasps were authorized for the Victory Medal, but bars were issued with the Occupation Medal to denote the recipient's area of service.

KOREA — The Korean Conflict, fought under the United Nations banner, added two new medals to the inventory. The first was the Korean Service Medal, which continued the practice of using 3/16" bronze stars on the ribbon to denote major engagements. The second, the National Defense Service Medal, set another record when it was later reinstated for the Vietnam and Gulf Wars to become the most awarded medal in U. S. history. Some units received the Korean Presidential Unit Citation and all participants were awarded the United Nations Service Medal, but no medal was ever issued by the South Korean Government to U. S. or other foreign troops.

U.S. Korean Service & United Nations Korean Service Medals

In the late 1950's and early 1960's, another substantial increase in awards took place as the Air Force, a separate service since 1947, created a flood of unique honors to replace their Army counterparts.

VIETNAM — The first American advisors in the Republic of South Vietnam, were awarded the new Armed Forces Expeditionary Medal which was created in 1961 to cover campaigns for which no specific medal was instituted. However, as the U. S. involvement in the Vietnamese conflict grew, a unique award, the Vietnam Service Medal was authorized, thus giving previous recipients of the Expeditionary medal the option of which medal to accept. The Government also authorized the acceptance of the Republic of Vietnam Campaign Medal by all who served for six months in-country, or in the surrounding waters or the air after 1960.

Asiatic-Pacific and European-African-Middle East Campaign Medals.

After Vietnam, many new decorations, medals and ribbons came into being as the Department of Defense and the individual Services developed a complete structure to reward performance from the newest enlistee to the most senior Pentagon Staffer. Some of the awards, such as the Army Service Ribbon and the Air Force Training Ribbon have little meaning, except to give the recruit something to wear on his chest. Conversely, the Achievement and Commendation Medals provide a useful means for a field commander to recognize younger individuals for outstanding performance.

U.S. Vietnam Service and RVN Campaign Medals.

GULF WAR — The conflict in the Gulf, as previously noted, saw the reinstitution of the National Defense Service Medal (this time it also covered the Reserves) and the creation of the Southwest Asia Service Medal for the personnel in theater. The Department of Defense also approved the wear of the Saudi Arabian Medal for the Liberation of Kuwait, which probably wins the award as the "Most Colorful Medal" hanging on any military chest. Recently the Department of Defense has also authorized the Kuwait Medal for the Liberation of Kuwait.

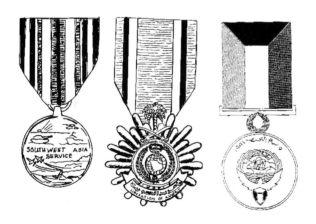

U. S. Southwest Asia Service Medal , Saudi Arabian Medal and the Kuwait Medal for Liberation of Kuwait

TYPE OF AWARDS — The terms, "Decoration" and "Medal" are used almost interchangeably today but there was once a recognizable distinction between them. Decorations, awarded for acts of valor and meritorious service, usually had distinctive (and often unique) shapes such as stars or crosses. Medals, which were awarded for participation in specific battles or campaigns, normally came in basic round. The fact that some very prestigious awards have the word "medal" in their titles

(e.g. <u>Medal</u> of Honor, Marine Corps Brevet <u>Medal</u>, Distinguished Service <u>Medal</u>, etc.) can cause some confusion to the novice.

Another type of award is a badge, indicating special proficiency in specific areas, such as marksmanship. The Services have also developed a system by which entire units, such as an Army Battalion or a Navy ship can be recognized for outstanding performance in the field. Members of the cited unit are entitled to wear an appropriate insignia representing the award (e.g.: Presidential Unit Citation, Navy Unit Commendation) or the French Fourragere, worn in perpetuity by members of many Army and Marine units to honor it's award during one of the World Wars.

PURPOSE — It is the purpose of this book to provide the reader with a clear road map of U. S. military awards and decorations. Starting on Page 9, details involved in claiming, wearing and displaying military awards are presented. The narrative continues on Page 16, with the personal decorations starting with the Medal of Honor and proceeding through the various levels of the "Pyramid of Honor". After personal decorations are the Good Conduct, Special Service and Reserve Meritorious Awards, followed by the service medals in chronological order from 1939 to present.

The Marksmanship medals and ribbons of the Navy, Coast Guard and Air Force are presented next (note that both the Army and Marine Corps award metal badges for shooting excellence, but these are beyond the scope of this book). This is followed by sections on the awards of various foreign governments to U. S. personnel, ribbons which have no associated medals ("ribbon only" awards) and, finally, U. S. and foreign unit awards.

Finally, to complete the awards picture, sections depicting the proper wear of ribbons, describing devices and attachments are included. Details of the U. S. awards systems for the various services complete the book.

From the earliest orders of knighthood to the present day commendations, the purpose of awards has always been twofold; the first is to promote good service, pride and courageous conduct among military personnel. The second is to create a mystique that will surround these symbols of a nation's appreciation and thus provides recognition for the recipients, their comrades and their families.

All the service medals and ribbons, and even the so-called "I Was There and Survived" awards have an important purpose. The display on a serviceman's chest can tell a commander at a glance the level of experience possessed by his subordinates. When a commander reviews his officers and NCO's, it only takes a minute or so to evaluate their backgrounds and predict performance from their ribbons.

It is, therefore, the authors' hope that this book will allow the reader, whether novice or veteran, to gain a new understanding of American Military awards, their evolution and history up to the present time.

3. CLAMING MILITARY MEDALS FROM THE U.S. GOVERNMENT

Veterans of any U. S. military service may request replacement of medals which have been lost, stolen, destroyed or rendered unfit through no fault of the recipient. Requests may also be filed for awards that were earned but, for any reason, were never issued to the service member. The next-of-kin of deceased veterans may also make the same request.

AIR FORCE — The Air Force processes requests for medals through the National Personnel Records Center, which determines eligibility through the information in the veteran's records. Once verified, a notification of entitlement is forwarded to Randolph Air Force Base, Texas, from which the medals are mailed to the requestor. To request medals earned while in the Air Force or its predecessor, the Army Air Corps, veterans or their next-of-kin should write to:

National Personnel Records Center
(Military Personnel Records)
9700 Page Avenue
St. Louis, MO 63132-5100

ARMY — The National Personnel Records Center does not determine eligibility for awards issued by the other services. If the person served in the Army, the request should be sent to:

U. S. Army Reserve Personnel Center
Attn.: ARPC-VSE-A (Medals)
9700 Page Avenue
St. Louis, MO 63132-5200

ALL NAVAL SERVICES — Requests pertaining to persons who served in the Navy, Marine Corps or Coast Guard should be sent to:

Navy Liaison Office (Navy medals)
Room 5409
9700 Page Avenue
St. Louis, MO 63132-5100

It is recommended that requesters use Standard Form 180, *Request Pertaining to Military Records*, when applying. Forms are available from offices of the Department of Veterans Affairs (VA) or photocopy the example on page 75. If the Standard Form 180 is not used, a letter may be sent, but it must include: the veteran's full name used while in service, the branch of service, approximate dates of service, and service number. The letter should indicate if the request is for a specific medal(s), or for all medals earned. The letter must be signed by the veteran or his next-of-kin, indicating the relationship to the deceased.

It is also helpful to include copies of any military service documents that indicate eligibility for medals, such as military orders or the veteran's report of separation (DD Form 214 or its earlier equivalent). This is especially important if the request pertains to one of the millions of veterans whose original records were lost in a fire at the National Personnel Records Center in 1973.

The fire destroyed 80 per cent of the Army discharge records between November 1912 and December 1959. World War II Army Air Corps discharge records are included in this group. Only five million Army discharge records remain from this period.

Seventy five per cent of Air Force discharge records before 1964 and whose last names that fall alphabetically between Hubbard (James E.) and Z were also burned. Only four million records from this period were saved. (Air Force records start in 1947 after it became a separate service from the Army.) Although the requested medals can often be issued on the basis of alternate records, the documents sent in with the request are sometimes the only means of determining proper eligibility.

Finally, requesters should exercise extreme patience. It may take several months or, in some cases, a year to determine eligibility and dispatch the appropriate medals.

The Bronze Star (Decoration), and The National Defense Service Medal (Medal)

4. PROPER WEAR OF U. S. AWARDS

WEAR ON CIVILIAN CLOTHES

There are two styles of awards that may be displayed on civilian clothes. The first is the small enameled lapel pin that represents the ribbon bar of a single decoration (usually the highest award or one having special meaning to the wearer). This is worn in the left lapel buttonhole of the civilian suit jacket. Many well-known veterans now in positions of leadership like Senator Bob Dole, a World War II Purple Heart recipient, wear such a lapel pin.

The other award style is the miniature medal, worn on the black or white dinner jacket at social functions. The rule of wear for these items is quite simple; if the lapel is wide enough, then they are worn on the lapel**. If the lapel is too narrow (e.g.: the shawl lapel on a tuxedo), the mini-medals are worn so that the bottom row of pendants just covers the top of the left breast pocket. No badges are ever worn on civilian dress.

** These are centered on the left lapel, 1/2 inch below the notch or 1 inch below the end of the collar gorge.

GENERAL CONSIDERATIONS

One of the earliest principles taught to the new recruit is that the uniform must always be worn properly. This applies to every item placed on that uniform, most especially to ribbons and medals. Decorations and awards must always be worn on the proper occasions, on the right uniform and in the correct order of precedence. The following pages outline the general rules for wear as prescribed by each Service. Regardless of branch, medals should always be clean and ribbons unsoiled. Items that are not absolutely spotless should <u>not</u> be worn, but should be redraped or reribboned immediately.

For active duty personnel, awards are worn per the applicable regulations on dress and service uniforms during normal working hours and while off-duty. Military personnel may also wear miniature medals on civilian evening attire at formal social functions.

National Guard and Reserve personnel follow the same general rules when in uniform. Those on the retired lists are also authorized to wear their uniforms and decorations on ceremonial occasions. This means a special event essentially military in nature at which the uniform is more appropriate than civilian dress. Examples of these are military balls, parades, weddings, funerals, memorial services, military association meetings and specific patriotic events. Military retirees may wear the uniform of their grade and branch at the time of retirement. However, military and civilian dress may not be mixed.

Retired personnel and former soldiers may wear either full size or miniature medals, on appropriate civilian clothing including clothes designed for veteran's and patriotic organizations on Veteran's Day, Memorial Day, and Armed Forces Day as well as at formal occasions of ceremony and social functions of a military nature.

<u>Miniature Medals shown near actual size.</u>

UNITED STATES ARMY

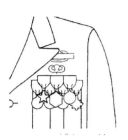

Wear Of Service Ribbons — Ribbons may be worn on the Army green, blue and white uniform coats. The ribbons are worn in one or more rows in order of precedence with either no space or 1/8 inch between rows, no more than four ribbons to a row. The top row is centered or aligned to left edge of the row underneath, whichever looks the best. Unit awards are centered above the right breast pocket.

Wear Of Full Size Decorations & Service Medals — Decorations and service medals may be worn on the Army blue or white uniform after retreat and by enlisted personnel on the dress green uniform for social functions. The medals are mounted in order of precedence, in rows with not more than four medals in a row. The top row cannot have more medals than the one below. Rows are separated by 1/8 inch. Medals may not overlap (as Navy and Marines do), so normally there are only three to a row due to the size of the coat. Service and training ribbons are not worn with full size medals.

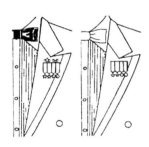

Wear Of Miniature Decorations & Service Medals — Miniature medals are scaled down replicas of full size medals. Only miniature medals are authorized for wear on the mess and evening uniform jackets (and with the blue and white uniform after retreat on formal occasions.)

Miniature medals are mounted on bars with the order of precedence from the wearer's right to left. The medals are mounted side by side if there are four or less. They may be overlapped up to 50% when five, six or seven are in a row. Overlapping is equal for all medals with the right one fully displayed. When two or more rows are worn, the bottom pendants must be fully visible.

UNITED STATES NAVY

(The USCG Generally Follows USN Guidelines)

Wear Of Service Ribbons — Wear up to 3 in a row; if more than three ribbons wear in horizontal rows of three each. The top row contains the lessor number, centered above the row below, no spaces between ribbon rows. Rows of ribbons covered by coat lapel may contain two ribbons each and be aligned. Wear ribbons with lower edge of bottom row centered 1/4 inch above left breast and parallel to the deck.

USCG member option is to either wear senior three ribbons or all ribbons when they are covered by lapel by 1/3 or more. Rows can be decreased to 2 or 1 if all ribbons are worn in this situation.

Wear Of Full Size Decorations And Service Medals — Wear large medals on full dress uniforms. Align bottom row same as ribbon bars. All rows may contain maximum of 3 medals side by side or up to 5 overlapping. Overlapping is proportional with inboard medal showing in full. Mount medals so they cover suspension ribbon of the medal below.

Wear Of Miniature Medals — Wear miniature medals with all formal and dinner dress uniforms. Place holding bar of lowest row of miniatures 3 inches below the notch, centered on the lapel. Center the holding bar immediately above the left breast pocket on the blue and white service coat. You may wear up to five miniature medals in a row with no overlap on the dinner jacket, center up to 3 miniature medals on the lapel. Position 4 or more miniatures at the inner edge of the lapel extending beyond the lapel to the body of the jacket.

UNITED STATES MARINE CORPS

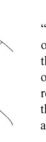

Wear Of Service Ribbons — Ribbons are authorized on Marine dress "B", dress "A" or shirts when prescribed as an outer garment. They are normally worn in rows of 3 or rows of 4 when displaying a large number of awards. If the lapel conceals any ribbons, they may be placed in successively decreasing rows (ie: 4, 3, 2, 1). All aligned vertically on center, except if the top row can be altered to present the neatest appearance. Ribbon rows may be spaced 1/8 inch apart or together. Ribbon bars are centered 1/8 inch above the upper left pocket. When marksmanship badges are worn, the ribbon bars are 1/8 inch above them.

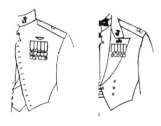

Full Size Medals — Marines wear up to 4 medals side by side on a 3 1/4 inch bar. A maximum of 7 medals may be overlapped (not to exceed 50% with the right or inboard medal shown in full). Full size medals are worn on blue or white dress coat centered on the left breast pocket with the upper edge of the holding bar on line midway between the 1st and 2nd button of the coat. When large medals are worn, all unit citations and ribbons with no medal authorized are centered over the right breast pocket the bottom edge 1/8 inch above the top of the pocket.

Wear Of Miniature Medals — When miniature medals are worn, no ribbons will be worn. On evening dress jackets miniature medals will be centered on the left front jacket panel midway between the inner edge and the left armhole seam, with the top of the bar on line with the 2nd blind button hole. On mess dress and SNCO's evening and mess dress the miniature medals are centered on the left lapel with the top of the holding bar 1 inch below the lapel notch.

UNITED STATES AIR FORCE

Wear Of Service Ribbons — Ribbons are worn on service dress and blue shirt. Ribbons are normally worn in rows of three with the bottom bar centered and resting on the top edge of the pocket. Ribbons may be worn four-in-a-row with the left edge of the ribbons aligned with the left edge of pocket to keep lapel from covering ribbons. There is no space between rows of ribbons.

Full Size Medals — Normally worn three to a row, but may be overlapped up to five medals on a 2 3/4 inch holding bar. No medal should be overlapped more than 50% and the medal nearest the lapel should be fully exposed. Six medals should be displayed in two rows, three over three. Regular size medals are worn on the service dress and ceremonial dress uniforms with the medal portion of the bottom row immediately above the top of the pocket button.

Miniature Medals — Miniature Medals are worn on the blue mess dress or on formal dress. The miniatures are centered between lapel and arm seam and midway between top shoulder seam and top button of jacket. If more than four miniatures, the wearer has the option of mounting up to seven by overlapping or going to a 2nd bar. Seven is the maximum on one bar, however, many in the Air Force prefer only a maximum of four to a bar.

5. HOW TO DISPLAY YOUR MEDALS

DISPLAYING MILITARY AWARDS

In the United States, it is quite rare for an individual to wear full-size medals once no longer on active duty. Unfortunately, many veterans return to civilian life with little concern for the state of their awards. In the euphoria of the moment, medals are tucked away in corners or children play with them, often causing irreparable damage to these noble mementos of a man's or woman's patriotic deeds. The loss or damage of these medals is sad, since awards reflect the veteran's part in American History and are totally unique and personal to each family.

The most appropriate use of military medals after active service is to mount the medals for permanent display in home or office. This reflects the individual's patriotism and the service rendered the United States. Unfortunately, there are very few first class companies in the United States who possess the expertise to properly prepare and mount awards and other personal militaria. The following pages provide examples of the formats, mounting methods and configurations employed by Medals of America, Limited in Fountain Inn, South Carolina to display military decorations. The examples range from a single medal to a dozen.

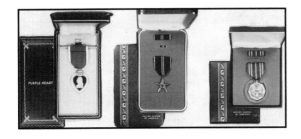

Decorations are usually awarded in a presentation set which normally consists of a medal, ribbon bar and lapel pin, all contained in a special case. During World War II, the name of the decoration was stamped in gold on the front of the case. However, as budget considerations assumed greater importance, this practice was gradually phased out and replaced by a standard case with "United States of America" emblazoned on the front.

At the present time, the more common decorations, (e.g., Achievement and Commendation Medals), come in small plastic cases, suitable only for initial presentation and storage of

the medal. Using this case in its open position for prolonged display exposes the entire presentation set to dust, acids and other atmospheric contaminants which can cause tarnish and/or serious discoloration.

Outside the case, medals and ribbons should be handled as little as possible, since oils and dirt on the hands can cause oxidation on the pendant and staining of the ribbon.

The most effective method of protecting awards involves the use of a shadow box or glass display case with at least 1/2 inch between the medals and the glass. This provides a three dimensional view and protects the medal display in a dust-free environment. Cases which press the medals and ribbons against the glass can disfigure the ribbon, cause discoloration and, in some extreme cases, damage the medal.

The greatest mistake an ordinary frame shop can make is in the actual process of mounting the medals. They often clip off prongs or pins on the back of a medal to ease the task of gluing the medal to a flat surface. The physical alteration destroys the integrity of the medal and the use of glues ruins the back of the ribbon and medal. The net result, ignoring the intrinsic value of the piece, is serious damage to a valued heirloom and keepsake.

The best way to mount medals is in a wooden case especially designed for that purpose. They can be obtained either with a fold-out easel back for placement on a table, desk or mantle, or with a notched hook on the rear of the wooden frame for hanging on a wall. The case should also have brass turnbuckles on the back to facilitate removal of the mounting board for close examination of the medals or rearrangement of the displayed items.

The mounting board is absolutely critical. Velvet, flannel and old uniforms, just don't do the job. A first class mounting system starts with acid-free Befang or Gator board at least 1/4 inch thick. This board is very sturdy, being composed of two layers of hard, white paper board sandwiched around a foam core. Over this, a high quality velour-type material to which velcro will adhere is glued and pressed down evenly. The medals are mounted using velcro tape; one piece over the ribbon mounting pin and one, about the size of a nickel, on the medal back. The velcro locks the medal very firmly into place without causing any damage and alleviates the need to cut off the pin backs. Badges or ribbon bars with pin backs can be mounted by pressing the prongs through the

13

fabric into the gator board, which moulds around the prongs. A little velcro tape on the back of the pronged device adds extra holding power.

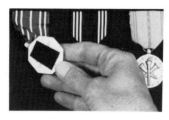

Patches, brass plates, dog tags and other mementos can easily be added this way. The great beauty of this method is found not only in its eye appeal, but also that one can add to the display or rearrange the existing contents by gently peeling the medal off as simply as opening a velcro zipper. Prong devices can also be moved easily, since the foam core closes in behind the prong as it is removed, thus effectively sealing the hole once more.

The final element in the process is the frame itself. While oak and other heavy woods make very handsome pieces of furniture, they are not a good choice for a frame. The frame's weight puts a great strain on modern plasterboard walls when an extensive medal display is attached via standard hooks and nails. In addition, handling a heavy frame by very young or very old hands increases the chance it could be accidentally dropped. For these reasons, frames should be milled from a lightweight wood with good staining characteristics. Bass wood is considered the best for the purpose and some poplar is acceptable. Metal frames, on the other hand, should be avoided, owing to their heavy weight and to the bright coloring which can conflict with the patina of the medals. Finally, the wood stain, (e.g., walnut stain), should reflect a rich, warm glow to properly envelop and enhance the medal display.

An essential part of the display case is the brass plate which provides the key information pertaining to the recipient of the displayed awards. This is definitely a place where one should <u>not</u> cut corners. A bargain basement brass or gold colored plastic nameplate will cheapen and distract from an otherwise elegant display case. Conversely, a high quality brass plate with good quality engraving will forever enhance the dignity of the medal display.

Whenever possible, the engraved letters should be blackened to provide enhanced contrast and visibility. The plate should, as a minimum, contain the full name, assigned unit and time frame. Other useful items are rank, service number and branch of the service if space permits. The contents of a nameplate are obviously a personal preference, but experience has shown that a limit of four or five lines can enhance and compliment the display, while greater numbers are a distraction.

Below and on the next page, are some examples of different display cases. The display of mounted miniature medals shown at right, is called a "convertible mount", since the entire group can be removed for wear. The flag case display below, allows a deceased veteran's flag, medals and photograph to be displayed as a lasting memorial.

A unique example of using ribbons, miniatures, medals and special badges.

This Air Force pilot's awards from Southwest Asia are mounted in a classic group of five. One more medal or badge requires a larger frame to prevent crowding.

These two cases show how a single or a few medals can be mounted in a handsome display.

A classic display of a WW II veteran's awards using his division patch as a focal point.

This Vietnam veteran used both of his combat patches so the overall composition is a nicely balanced inverted "V".

This WW II Navy veteran uses his rating badge as a very effective focal point.

This Korean War Marine uses his combat patch, and dress collar insignia over the medals. The small rank badge and shooting badges flanking the name plate present a wonderful picture of his military service.

World War II Army Air Corps Display

6. U.S. MILITARY AWARDS

THE PYRAMID OF HONOR

The awards system of the United States as described in the introduction, has evolved into a structured program often called the "Pyramid of Honor". The system is designed to reward services ranging from heroism on the battlefield to superior performance of non-combat duties and even includes the completion of entry level training.

Far from being disturbed by the award proliferation, the Armed Services have embraced Napoleon's concept of liberally awarding medals to enhance morale and esprit de corps. This expanded and specially-tailored awards program is generally very popular in the all-volunteer armed forces and has played a significant part in improving morale, job performance, recruitment and re-enlistments amongst junior officers and enlisted personnel.

The decorations and awards which represent the rich American military heritage from 1939 onward are presented on the following pages in an overall order of precedence (individual Service orders of precedence start on page 38). These awards paint a wonderful portrait of this country's dedication to the ideals of freedom and the honors and sacrifices required of the military to support those ideals.

It is to be noted that in the following award descriptions, the numbers in parentheses on the "Device" line refer to the tables contained in the "Attachments and Devices" section, starting on page 51.

THE MEDAL OF HONOR

In a country whose Government is based on a totally democratic society, it is fitting that the first medal to reward meritorious acts on the field of battle should be for private soldiers and seamen (although extended in later years to officers).

The Congressional Medal of Honor (referred to universally as the "Medal of Honor" in all statutes, awards manuals and uniform regulations) was born in conflict, steeped in controversy during its early years and finally emerged, along with Britain's Victoria Cross and France's Legion of Honor, as one of the world's premier awards for bravery.

The medal is actually a statistical oddity, proving the unlikely equation that "Three equals One". Although there are three separate medals representing America's highest reward for bravery (illustrated as items **1**, **2** and **3** on the next page) there is now only a single set of directives governing the award of this, the most coveted of all U.S. decorations.

The medal was created during the Civil War as a reward for "gallantry in action and other soldierlike qualities" ("...seamanlike qualities..." in the case of the Navy). However, the reference to "other qualities" led to many awards for actions which would seem less than heroic, including the bestowal of 864 awards upon the entire membership of the 27th Maine Volunteer Infantry for merely reenlisting.

The inconsistencies in those and other dubious cases, were apparently resolved in the early 20th Century when 910 names were removed from the lists (including the 864 of the 27th Maine). At the same time, the statutes which govern the award of the medal were revised to reflect the present-day criteria of "Conspicuous gallantry and intrepidity at the risk of one's own life above and beyond the call of duty."

ARMY MEDAL OF HONOR

The Army Medal of Honor was first awarded in 1862 but, owing to extensive copying by veterans groups, was redesigned in 1904 and patented by the War Department to ensure the design exclusivity.

The medal, a five pointed golden star, lays over a green enamelled laurel wreath. The center of the star depicts the head of Minerva, Goddess of righteous war and wisdom, encircled by the words: "United States of America". The back of the medal is inscribed: "The Congress to" with a place for the recipient's name. The medal hangs from a bar inscribed "Valor" which is held by an American Eagle with laurel leaves (denoting peace) in its right talon and arrows (war) in its left. The eagle is fastened by a hook to a light blue pad on which are embroidered 13 white stars.

NAVY MEDAL OF HONOR

The 1861 Navy Medal of Honor was redesigned by Tiffany in 1917 but was returned to the basic 1861 design in 1942 and a neck ribbon added. The design is a five point bronze star with a central circular plaque depicting Minerva repulsing discord. The reverse is engraved "Personal Valor" with room for the recipient's name, rank, ship or unit and date. The medal hangs from the flukes of an anchor which is attached to the neck ribbon.

AIR FORCE MEDAL OF HONOR

Congress established the Air Force Medal of Honor in 1960, 13 years after the establishment of the Air Force as an independent Service (prior to 1960, airmen received the Army medal). The medal design was fashioned after the Army version and is a five pointed star with a green enamelled laurel wreath. The center depicts the head of the Statue of Liberty surrounded by 34 stars. The star hangs from a representation of the Air Force coat of arms and is suspended from a bar inscribed "Valor".

Plate 1. MEDALS OF HONOR

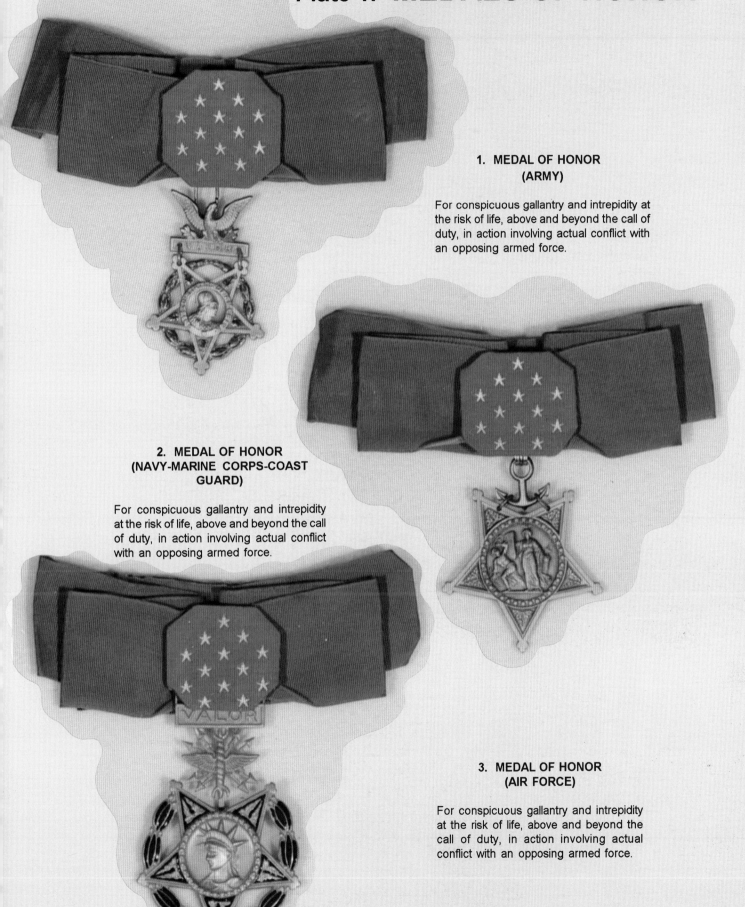

**1. MEDAL OF HONOR
(ARMY)**

For conspicuous gallantry and intrepidity at the risk of life, above and beyond the call of duty, in action involving actual conflict with an opposing armed force.

**2. MEDAL OF HONOR
(NAVY-MARINE CORPS-COAST
GUARD)**

For conspicuous gallantry and intrepidity at the risk of life, above and beyond the call of duty, in action involving actual conflict with an opposing armed force.

**3. MEDAL OF HONOR
(AIR FORCE)**

For conspicuous gallantry and intrepidity at the risk of life, above and beyond the call of duty, in action involving actual conflict with an opposing armed force.

Plate 2. U.S. Personal Decorations - Sheet 1

4. Distinguished Service Cross

5. Navy Cross

6. Air Force Cross

7. Defense Distinguished Service Medal

8. Army Distinguished Service Medal

9. Navy Distinguished Service Medal

10. Air Force Distinguished Service Medal

11. Coast Guard Distinguished Service Medal

12. Silver Star

13. Defense Superior Service Medal

14. Legion Of Merit

15. Dist. Flying Cross

4. Distinguished Service Cross Service: Army Instituted: 1918 Criteria: Extraordinary heroism in action against an enemy of the U.S. while engaged in military operations involving conflict with an opposing foreign force or while serving with friendly foreign forces Devices: Bronze, silver oak leaf cluster (28, 32) Notes: 100 copies of earlier design cross issued with a European-style (unedged) ribbon ("French Cut")	**5. Navy Cross** Service: Navy/Marine Corps/Coast Guard Instituted: 1919 Criteria: Extraordinary heroism in action against an enemy of the U.S. while engaged in military operations involving conflict with an opposing foreign force or while serving with friendly foreign forces Devices: Gold, silver star (66, 70) Notes: Originally issued with a 1 1/2" wide ribbon	**6. Air Force Cross** Service: Air Force Instituted: 1960 Criteria: Extraordinary heroism in action against an enemy of the U.S. while engaged in military operations involving conflict with an opposing foreign force or while serving with friendly foreign forces Devices: Bronze, silver oak leaf cluster (28, 32) Notes: Created under the same legislation which established the Distinguished Service Cross 42 years earlier	**7. Defense Distinguished Service Medal** Service: All Services (by Secretary of Defense) Instituted: 1970 Criteria: Exceptionally meritorious service to the United States while assigned to a Joint Activity in a position of unique and great responsibility Devices: Army/Air Force/Navy/Marine Corps: bronze & silver oak leaf cluster (29, 33); Coast Guard: gold, silver star (65, 69) Notes: The oak leaf cluster may not be worn on the Coast Guard uniform
8. Army Distinguished Service Medal Service: Army Instituted: 1918 Criteria: Exceptionally meritorious service to the United States Government in a duty of great responsibility Devices: Bronze, silver oak leaf cluster (28, 32) Notes: Originally issued with European (unedged) ribbon ("French Cut")	**9. Navy Distinguished Service Medal** Service: Navy/Marine Corps Instituted: 1919 Criteria: Exceptionally meritorious service to the United States Government in a duty of great responsibility Devices: Gold, silver star (66, 70) Notes: 107 copies of earlier medal design issued but later withdrawn. First ribbon design was 1 1/2" wide	**10. Air Force Distinguished Service Medal** Service: Air Force Instituted: 1960 Criteria: Exceptionally meritorious service to the United States Government in a duty of great responsibility Devices: Bronze, silver oak leaf cluster (28, 32) Notes: Original design was modified and used as the Airman's Medal	**11. Coast Guard Distinguished Service Medal** Service: Coast Guard Instituted: 1961 Criteria: Exceptionally meritorious service to the United States Government in a duty of great responsibility Devices: Gold, silver star (66, 70) Notes: Originally authorized in 1949 but the design was not approved until 1961
12. Silver Star Service: All Services (originally Army only) Instituted: 1932 Criteria: Gallantry in action against an armed enemy of the United States or while serving with friendly foreign forces Devices: Army/Air Force: bronze, silver oak leaf cluster (28, 32); Navy/Marine Corps/Coast Guard: gold, silver star (66, 70) Notes: Derived from the 3/16" silver "Citation Star" previously worn on Army campaign medals	**13. Defense Superior Service Medal** Service: All Services (by Secretary of Defense) Instituted: 1970 Criteria: Superior meritorious service to the United States while assigned to a Joint Activity in a position of significant responsibility Devices: Army/Air Force/Navy/Marine Corps: bronze, silver oak leaf cluster (29, 33); Coast Guard: gold, silver star (65, 69) Notes: Oak leaf cluster not worn on Coast Guard uniform	**14. Legion of Merit** Service: All Services Instituted: 1942 Criteria: Exceptionally meritorious conduct in the performance of outstanding services to the United States Devices: Army/Air Force: bronze, silver oak leaf cluster (28, 32); Navy/Marine Corps/Coast Guard: bronze letter "V" (for valor) (17), gold, silver star (66, 70) Notes: Issued in four degrees (Legionnaire, Officer, Commander & Chief Commander) to foreign nationals	**15. Distinguished Flying Cross** Service: All Services Instituted: 1926 Criteria: Heroism or extraordinary achievement while participating in aerial flight Devices: Army/Air Force: bronze, silver oak leaf cluster (28, 32); Navy/Marine Corps: bronze letter "V" (for valor) (17), gold, silver star (66, 70); Coast Guard: gold, silver star (66, 70)

Plate 2. U.S. Personal Decorations - Sheet 2

16. Soldier's Medal

17. Navy and Marine Corps Medal

18. Airman's Medal

19. Coast Guard

20. Gold Lifesaving Medal

21. Bronze Star Medal

22. Purple Heart

23. Defense Meritorious Service Medal

24. Meritorious Service

25. Air Medal

26. Silver Lifesaving Medal

27. Aerial Achievement

16. Soldier's Medal Service: Army Instituted: 1926 Criteria: Heroism not involving actual conflict with an armed enemy of the United States Devices: Bronze, silver oak leaf cluster (28, 32) Notes: Award requires personal hazard or danger and voluntary risk of life	**17. Navy and Marine Corps Medal** Service: Navy/Marine Corps Instituted: 1942 Criteria: Heroism not involving actual conflict with an armed enemy of the United States Devices: Gold, silver star (66, 70) Notes: For acts of life-saving, action must be at great risk to one's own life	**18. Airman's Medal** Service: Air Force Instituted: 1960 Criteria: Heroism involving voluntary risk of life under conditions other than those of actual conflict with an armed enemy Devices: Bronze, silver oak leaf cluster (28, 32) Notes: Derived from original design of Air Force Distinguished Service Medal	**19. Coast Guard Medal** Service: Coast Guard Instituted: 1958 Criteria: Heroism not involving actual conflict with an armed enemy of the United States Devices: Gold, silver star (66, 70) Notes: Authorized in 1949 but not designed and issued until 1958
20. Gold Life Saving Medal Service: All Services and Civilians Instituted: 1874 (modified 1882 and 1946) Criteria: Heroic conduct at the risk of life during the rescue or attempted rescue of a victim of drowning or shipwreck Devices: Coast Guard: gold star (66) Notes: Normally a "Non-Military Decoration" but considered a personal decoration by the Coast Guard. Originally a "table" (non-wearable) medal then worn with a 2" wide ribbon	**21. Bronze Star Medal** Service: All Services Instituted: 1944 Criteria: Heroic or meritorious achievement or service not involving participation in aerial flight Devices: Army/Air Force: bronze letter "V" (for valor) (17), bronze, silver oak leaf cluster (28, 32); Navy/Marine Corps/Coast Guard: bronze letter "V" (for valor) (17), gold, silver star (66, 70) Notes: Awarded to World War II holders of Army Combat Infantryman Badge or Combat Medical Badge	**22. Purple Heart** Service: All Services (originally Army only) Instituted: 1932 Criteria: Awarded to any member of the U.S. Armed Forces killed or wounded in an armed conflict Devices: Army/Air Force: bronze, silver oak leaf cluster (28, 32); Navy/Marine Corps/Coast Guard: gold, silver star (66, 70) Notes: Wound Ribbon appeared circa 1917-18 but was never officially authorized. (Army used wound chevrons during World War I)	**23. Defense Meritorious Service Medal** Service: All Services (by Secretary of Defense) Instituted: 1977 Criteria: Noncombat meritorious achievement or service while assigned to the Joint Activity Devices: Army/Air Force/Navy/Marine Corps: bronze, silver oak leaf cluster (29, 33); Coast Guard: gold, silver star (65, 69) Notes: Coast Guard uses gold star device since the oak leaf cluster may not be worn on its uniform
24. Meritorious Service Medal Service: All Services Instituted: 1969 Criteria: Outstanding noncombat meritorious achievement or service to the United States Devices: Army/Air Force: bronze, silver oak leaf cluster (28, 32); Navy/Marine Corps: gold, silver star (66, 70); Coast Guard: silver letter "O" (14), gold, silver star (66, 70)	**25. Air Medal** Service: All Services Instituted: 1942 Criteria: Heroic actions or meritorious service while participating in aerial flight Devices: Army: bronze letter "V" (for valor) (17), bronze numeral (25); Air Force: bronze, silver oak leaf cluster (28, 32); Navy/Marine Corps: bronze letter "V" (for valor) (17), bronze numeral (21), gold numeral (26), bronze star (53), gold, silver star (66, 70); Coast Guard: gold, silver star (66, 70)	**26. Silver Life Saving Medal** Service: All Services and Civilians Instituted: 1874 (modified 1882 and 1946) Criteria: Heroic conduct during rescue or attempted rescue of a victim of drowning or shipwreck Devices: Coast Guard: gold star (66) Notes: Normally a "Non-Military Decoration" but considered a personal decoration by the Coast Guard. Originally a "table" (non-wearable) medal then worn with a 2" wide ribbon	**27. Aerial Achievement Medal** Service: Air Force Instituted: 1988 Criteria: Sustained meritorious achievement while participating in aerial flight Devices: Bronze, silver oak leaf cluster (28, 32) Notes: Considered on a par with the Air Medal but more likely to be awarded for peacetime actions

Plate 2. U.S. Personal Decorations - Sheet 3

28. Joint Service
Commendation Medal

29. Army Commendation
Medal

30. Navy Commendation
Medal

31. Air Force Commenda-
tion Medal

32. Coast Guard
Commendation Medal

33. Joint Service
Achievement Medal

34. Army Achievement
Medal

35. Navy Achievement
Medal

38. Commandant's Letter
Of Commendation Ribbon

39. Combat Action
Ribbon

36. Air Force Achievement
Medal

37. Coast Guard
Achievement Medal

28. Joint Service Commendation Medal	29. Army Commendation Medal	30. Navy & Marine Corps Commendation Medal	31. Air Force Commendation Medal
Service: All Services (by Secretary of Defense)	Service: Army	Service: Navy/Marine Corps	Service: Air Force
Instituted: 1963	Instituted: 1945 (retroactive to 1941)	Instituted: 1944 (retroactive to 1941)	Instituted: 1958
Criteria: Meritorious service or achievement while assigned to a Joint Activity	Criteria: Heroism, meritorious achievement or meritorious service	Criteria: Heroic or meritorious achievement or service	Criteria: Outstanding achievement or meritorious service rendered on behalf of the United States Air Force and, where appropriate, unusual and extraordinarily sustained meritorious performance by aircrew members
Devices: Army/Air Force/ Navy/Marine Corps: bronze letter "V" (for valor) (17), bronze, silver oak leaf cluster (29, 33); Coast Guard: bronze letter "V" (for valor), gold, silver star (65, 69)	Devices: Bronze letter "V" (for valor) (17), bronze, silver oak leaf cluster (28, 32)	Devices: Bronze letter "V" (for valor) (17), gold, silver star (66, 70)	Devices: Bronze, silver oak leaf cluster (28, 32)
Notes: Coast Guard uses gold star device since the oak leaf cluster may not be worn on its uniform	Notes: Originally a ribbon-only award then designated "Army Commendation Ribbon with Metal Pendant". Redesignated: "Army Commendation Medal" in 1960	Notes: Originally a ribbon-only award then designated "Navy Commendation Ribbon with Metal Pendant". Redesignated: "Navy Commendation Medal" in 1960. Change to present name was made in 1994	

32. Coast Guard Commendation Medal	33. Joint Service Achievement Medal	34. Army Achievement Medal	35. Navy & Marine Corps Achievement Medal
Service: Coast Guard	Service: All Services (by Secretary of Defense)	Service: Army	Service: Navy/Marine Corps
Instituted: 1947	Instituted: 1983	Instituted: 1981	Instituted: 1961
Criteria: 1. Heroic or meritorious achievement or service. 2. Meritorious service resulting in unusual or outstanding achievement	Criteria: Meritorious service or achievement while serving with a Joint Activity	Criteria: Meritorious service or achievement while serving in a non-combat area	Criteria: Meritorious service or achievement in a combat or noncombat situation based on sustained performance of a superlative nature
Devices: Silver letter "O" (14), bronze letter "V" (for valor) (17), gold, silver star (66, 70)	Devices: Army/Air Force/ Navy/Marine Corps: bronze, silver oak leaf cluster (29, 33); Coast Guard: gold, silver star (65, 69)	Devices: Bronze, silver oak leaf cluster (28, 32)	Devices: Bronze letter "V" (for valor) (17), gold, silver star (66, 70)
Notes: Originally "Commendation Ribbon with Metal Pendant". Redesignated: "Coast Guard Commendation Medal" in 1959	Notes: Coast Guard uses gold star device since the oak leaf cluster may not be worn on its uniform	Notes: Intended for Company grade officers and enlisted grades E-6 and below	Notes: Originally a ribbon-only award: "Secretary of the Navy Commendation for Achievement Award with Ribbon". Changed to present form in 1967. Changed to present name in 1994

36. Air Force Achievement Medal	37. Coast Guard Achievement Medal	38. Commandant's Letter of Commendation Ribbon	39. Combat Action Ribbon
Service: Air Force	Service: Coast Guard	Service: Coast Guard	Service: Navy/Marine Corps
Instituted: 1980	Instituted: 1964	Instituted: 1979	Instituted: 1969
Criteria: Outstanding achievement or meritorious service not warranting award of the Air Force Commendation Medal	Criteria: Professional and/or leadership achievement in a combat or noncombat situation	Criteria: Receipt of a letter of commendation for an act or service resulting in unusual and/or outstanding achievement	Criteria: Active participation in ground or air combat during specifically listed military operations
Devices: Bronze, silver oak leaf cluster (28, 32)	Devices: Silver letter "O" (14), bronze letter "V" (for valor) (17), gold, silver star (66, 70)	Devices: Silver letter "O" (14), gold, silver star (66, 70)	Devices: Gold, silver star (66, 70)
	Notes: Originally a ribbon-only award. Present configuration adopted in 1968		Notes: This is the only Navy personal decoration which has no associated medal (a "ribbon-only: award)

Plate 3. U.S. Special Service, Good Conduct & Reserve Awards

40. Prisoner Of War Medal

41. Combat Readiness Medal

42. Army Good Conduct Medal

43. Navy Good Condu... Medal

44. Marine Corps Good Conduct Medal

45. Air Force Good Conduct Medal

46. Coast Guard Good Conduct Medal

47. Reserve Good Co... duct Medal

48. Army Reserve Components Achievment Medal

49. Naval Reserve Meritorious Service Medal

50. Air Reserve Forces Meritorious Service Medal

51. Selected Marine Corps Reserve Medal

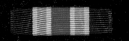

52. Fleet Marine Force

53. Outstanding Airman of

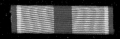

54. Air Force Recognition

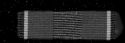

55. Navy Reserve Spec...

Special Service, Good Conduct & Reserve Meritorious Awards

40. Prisoner of War Medal Service: All Services Instituted: 1989 Criteria: Awarded to any member of the U.S. Armed Forces taken prisoner during any armed conflict dating from World War I Devices: Bronze, silver star (49, 59)	**41. Combat Readiness Medal** Service: Air Force Instituted: 1964 Criteria: Awarded for specific periods of qualifying service in a combat or mission-ready status Devices: Bronze, silver oak leaf cluster (27, 31)	**42. Army Good Conduct Medal** Service: Army Instituted: 1941 Criteria: Exemplary conduct, efficiency and fidelity during three years of active enlisted service with the U.S. Army (1 year during wartime) Devices: Bronze, silver, gold knotted bar (4)	**43. Navy Good Conduct Medal** Service: Navy Instituted: 1888 Criteria: Outstanding performance and conduct during 4 years of continuous active enlisted service Devices: Bronze, silver star (52, 60) Notes: Earlier ribbon was a brighter shade of red
44. Marine Corps Good Conduct Medal Service: Marine Corps Instituted: 1896 Criteria: Outstanding performance and conduct during 3 years of continuous active enlisted service in the U.S. Marine Corps Devices: Bronze, silver star (52, 60) Notes: Earlier ribbon was 1 1/4" wide	**45. Air Force Good Conduct Medal** Service: Air Force Instituted: 1953 Criteria: Exemplary conduct, efficiency and fidelity during three years of active enlisted service with the U.S. Air Force Devices: Bronze, silver oak leaf cluster (28, 32)	**46. Coast Guard Good Conduct Medal** Service: Coast Guard Instituted: 1921 Criteria: Outstanding proficiency, leadership and conduct during 3 continuous years of active enlisted Coast Guard service Devices: Bronze, silver star (55, 61) Notes: Earlier ribbon was 1 1/2" wide	**47. Coast Guard Reserve Good Conduct Medal** Service: Coast Guard Instituted: 1963 Criteria: Outstanding proficiency, leadership and conduct during 3 years of enlisted service in the Coast Guard Reserve Devices: Bronze, silver star (55, 61) Notes: Originally a ribbon-only award- "Coast Guard Reserve Meritorious Service Ribbon"
48. Army Reserve Components Achievement Medal Service: Army Instituted: 1971 Criteria: Exemplary conduct, efficiency and fidelity during 4 years of enlisted service with the U.S. Army Reserve or National Guard Devices: Bronze, silver oak leaf cluster (28, 32)	**49. Naval Reserve Meritorious Service Medal** Service: Navy Instituted: 1964 Criteria: Outstanding performance and conduct during 4 years of enlisted service in the Naval Reserve Devices: Bronze, silver star (52, 60) Notes: Originally a ribbon-only award.	**50. Air Reserve Forces Meritorious Service Medal** Service: Air Force Instituted: 1964 Criteria: Exemplary behavior, efficiency and fidelity during three years of active enlisted service with the Air Force Reserve Devices: Bronze, silver oak leaf cluster (28, 32)	**51. Selected Marine Corps Reserve Medal** Service: Marine Corps Instituted: 1939 Criteria: Outstanding performance and conduct during 4 years of enlisted service in the Marine Corps Selected Reserve Devices: Bronze, silver star (52, 60) Notes: Formerly: "Organized Marine Corps Reserve Medal"
52. Fleet Marine Force Ribbon Service: Navy Instituted: 1984 Criteria: Active participation by professionally skilled Navy personnel with the Fleet Marine Force Devices: None	**53. Outstanding Airman of the Year Ribbon** Service: Air Force Instituted: 1968 Criteria: Awarded to airmen for selection to the "12 Outstanding Airmen of the Year" Competition Program Devices: Bronze, silver oak leaf cluster (27, 31), bronze star (50)	**54. Air Force Recognition Ribbon** Service: Air Force Instituted: 1980 Criteria: Awarded to individual recipients of Air Force-level special trophies and awards Devices: Bronze, silver oak leaf cluster (27, 31)	**55. Navy Reserve Special Commendation Ribbon (obsolete)** Service: Navy/Marine Corps Instituted: 1946 Criteria: Awarded to Reserve Officers with 4 years of successful command and a total Reserve service of 10 years Devices: None

Plate 4. U.S. Service Medals - Sheet 1

56. Navy Expeditionary
Medal

57. Marine Corps
Expeditionary Medal

58. China Service Medal

59. American Defense
Service Medal

60. Women's Army Corps
Service Medal

61. American Campaign
Medal

62. Asiatic-Pacific
Campaign Medal

63. European-African-
Middle Eastern
Campaign Medal

64. World War II Victory
Medal

65. U. S. Antarctic
Expedition Medal

66. Army of Occupation
Medal

67. Navy Occupation
Medal

56. Navy Expeditionary Medal Service: Navy Instituted: 1936 Dates: 1936 to Present Criteria: Landings on foreign territory and operations against armed opposition for which no specific campaign medal has been authorized Devices: Silver letter "W" (19) (denotes bar below), bronze, silver star (52, 60) Bar: "Wake Island" (see pages 58-59)	**57. Marine Corps Expeditionary Medal** Service: Marine Corps Instituted: 1919 Dates: 1919 to Present Criteria: Landings on foreign territory and operations against armed opposition for which no specific campaign medal has been authorized Devices: Silver letter "W" (19) (denotes bar below), bronze, silver star (52, 60) Notes: Originally a "ribbon-only" award Bar: "Wake Island" (see pages 58-59)	**58. China Service Medal** Service: Navy/Marine Corps/Coast Guard Instituted: 1940 Dates: 1937-39, 1945-57 Criteria: Service ashore in China or on-board naval vessels during either of the above periods Devices: Bronze star (54) Notes: Medal was reinstituted in 1947 for extended service during dates shown above	**59. American Defense Service Medal** Service: All Services Instituted: 1941 Dates: 1939-41 Criteria: Army: 12 months of active duty service during the above period; Naval Services: Any active duty service Devices: All Services: bronze star (48) (denotes bars below); All Naval Services: bronze letter "A" (8) (not worn with bronze star [device no.48] above) Bars: "Foreign Service", "Base", "Fleet", "Sea" (see pages 58-59)
60. Women's Army Corps Service Medal Service: Army Instituted: 1943 Dates: 1941-46 Criteria: Service with both the Women's Army Auxiliary Corps and Women's Army Corps during the above period Devices: None Notes: Only U.S. award authorized for women only.	**61. American Campaign Medal** Service: All Services Instituted: 1942 Dates: 1941-46 Criteria: Service outside the U.S. in the American theater for 30 days, or within the continental U.S. for one year. Devices: All Services: bronze, silver star (46, 58); Navy: bronze Marine Corps device (20); Navy/Marine Corps: silver star (72) (obsolete)	**62. Asiatic-Pacific Campaign Medal** Service: All Services Instituted: 1942 Dates: 1941-46 Criteria: Service in the Asiatic-Pacific theater for 30 day or receipt of any combat decoration Devices: All Services: bronze, silver star (46, 58); Army/Air Force: bronze arrowhead (2); Navy: bronze Marine Corps device (20); Navy/Marine Corps: silver star (72) (obsolete)	**63. European-African-Middle Eastern Campaign Medal** Service: All Services Instituted: 1942 Dates: 1941-45 Criteria: Service in the European-African-Middle Eastern theater for 30 days or receipt of any combat decoration Devices: All Services: bronze, silver star (46, 58); Army/Air Force: bronze arrowhead (2); Navy: bronze Marine Corps device (20); Navy/Marine Corps: silver star (72) (obsolete)
64. World War II Victory Medal Service: All Services Instituted: 1945 Dates: 1941-46 Criteria: Awarded for service in the U.S. Armed Forces during the above period Devices: None	**65. U.S. Antarctic Expedition Medal** Service: Navy/Coast Guard Instituted: 1945 Dates: 1939-41 Criteria: Awarded in gold, silver and bronze to members of the U.S. Antarctic Expedition of 1939-41 Devices: None	**66. Army of Occupation Medal** Service: Army/Air Force Instituted: 1946 Dates: 1945-55 (Berlin: 1945-90) Criteria: 30 consecutive days of service in occupied territories of former enemies during above period Devices: Gold airplane (1) Bars: "Germany", "Japan" (see pages 58-59)	**67. Navy Occupation Medal** Service: Navy/Marine Corps/Coast Guard Instituted: 1948 Dates: 1945-55 (Berlin: 1945-90) Criteria: 30 consecutive days of service in occupied territories of former enemies during above period Devices: Gold airplane (1) Bars: "Europe", "Asia" (see pages 58-59)

Plate 4. U.S. Service Medals - Sheet 2

68. Medal for Humane Action

69. National Defense Service Medal

70. Korean Service Medal

71. Antarctica Service Medal

72. Arctic Service Medal

73. Armed Forces Expeditionary Medal

74. Vietnam Service Medal

75. Southwest Asia Service Medal

76. Armed Forces Service Medal

77. Humanitarian Service Medal

78. Outstanding Volunteer Service Medal

79. Armed Forces Reserve Medal

80. Naval Reserve Medal (obsolete)

68. Medal for Humane Action

Service: All Services

Instituted: 1949

Dates: 1948-49

Criteria: 120 consecutive days of service participating in the Berlin Airlift or in support thereof. Was also awarded posthumously

Devices: None

Note: Sometimes confused with the Humanitarian Service Medal (established in 1977) but was only awarded for Berlin Airlift service

69. National Defense Service Medal

Service: All Services

Instituted: 1953

Dates: 1950-54, 1961-74, 1990-95

Criteria: Any honorable active duty service during any of the above periods

Devices: All Services: bronze star (44); Army: bronze oak leaf cluster (30) (obsolete)

Notes: Reinstituted in 1966 and 1991 for Vietnam and Southwest Asia (Gulf War) actions respectively

70. Korean Service Medal

Service: All Services

Instituted: 1950

Dates: 1950-54

Criteria: Participation in military operations within the Korean area during the above period

Devices: All Services: bronze, silver star (46, 58); Army/Air Force: bronze arrowhead (2); Navy: bronze Marine Corps device (20)

71. Antarctica Service Medal

Service: All Services

Instituted: 1960

Dates: 1946 to Present

Criteria: 30 calendar days of service on the Antarctic Continent

Devices: Bronze, gold, silver disks (5) (denote bars below)

Bars: "Wintered Over" in bronze, gold, silver (see pages 58-59)

72. Arctic Service Medal

Service: Coast Guard

Instituted: 1976

Dates: 1946 to Present

Criteria: Awarded for 21 days of service on vessels operating in polar waters north of the Arctic Circle

Devices: For all deployments after 1 January 1989: bronze, silver star (55, 61)

73. Armed Forces Expeditionary Medal

Service: All Services

Instituted: 1961

Dates: 1958 to Present

Criteria: Participation in military operations not covered by specific war medal

Devices: All Services: bronze, silver star (46, 58); Army: bronze arrowhead (2); Navy: bronze Marine Corps device (20)

Notes: Was awarded for service in Vietnam until establishment of Vietnam Service Medal

74. Vietnam Service Medal

Service: All Services

Instituted: 1965

Dates: 1965-73

Criteria: Service in Vietnam, Laos, Cambodia or Thailand during the above period

Devices: All Services: bronze, silver star (46, 58); Army: bronze arrowhead (2); Navy: bronze Marine Corps device (20)

75. Southwest Asia Service Medal

Service: All Services

Instituted: 1992

Dates: 1991 to Present

Criteria: Active participation in, or support of, Operations Desert Shield and/or Desert Storm

Devices: All Services: bronze star (46); Navy: bronze Marine Corps device (20)

Notes: Terminal date of service not established as of the date of this writing

76. Armed Forces Service Medal

Service: All Services

Instituted: 1995

Dates: 1995 to Present

Criteria: Participation in military operations not covered by a specific war medal or the Armed Forces Expeditionary Medal

Devices: All Services: bronze, silver star (49, 59)

77. Humanitarian Service Medal

Service: All Services

Instituted: 1977

Dates: 1975 to Present

Criteria: Direct participation in specific operations of a humanitarian nature

Devices: All Services: bronze, silver star (49, 59); Army/Air Force/ Navy/Marine Corps: bronze numeral (22) (obsolete)

78. Outstanding Volunteer Service Medal

Service: All Services

Instituted: 1993

Dates: 1993 to Present

Criteria: Awarded for outstanding and sustained voluntary service to the civilian community

Devices: All Services: bronze, silver star (49, 59)

79. Armed Forces Reserve Medal

Service: All Services

Instituted: 1950

Dates: 1949 to Present

Criteria: 10 years of honorable service in any reserve component of the United States Armed Forces Reserve

Devices: Bronze hourglass (7), bronze letter "M" (12A)

80. Naval Reserve Medal (obsolete)

Service: Navy

Instituted: 1938

Dates: 1938-58

Criteria: 10 years of honorable service in the U.S. Naval Reserve

Devices: Bronze star (52)

Notes: Replaced by Armed Forces Reserve Medal (No. 79 at left). Some earlier versions had deep red ribbon.

Plate 5. U.S. Marksmanship Awards

81. Navy Expert Rifleman Medal

82. Navy Expert Pistol Shot Medal

83. Navy Rifle Marksmanship Ribbon

84. Navy Pistol Marksmanship Ribbon

85. Navy Distinguished Marksman Ribbon (0)

86. Navy Distinguished Pistol Shot Ribbon (0)

87. Navy Distinguished Marksman and Pistol Shot Ribbon (Obsolete)

88. Air Force Small Arms Expert Marksmanship Ribbon

88a. Air Force Small Arms Expert Marksmanship Ribbon (With Device)

89. Coast Guard Expert Rifleman Medal

90. Coast Guard Expert Pistol Shot

91. Coast Guard Rifle Marksmanship Ribbon

92. Coast Guard Pistol Marksmanship Ribbon

91a. Coast Guard Rifle Marksmanship Ribbon

(With Devices)

92a. Coast Guard Pistol Marksmanship Ribbon

(With Devices)

30

81. Navy Expert Rifleman Medal

Service: Navy

Criteria: Attainment of the minimum qualifying score for the expert level during prescribed shooting exercises

Devices: None on medal (but see item 82)

---

82. Navy Expert Pistol Shot Medal

Service: Navy

Criteria: Attainment of the minimum qualifying score for the expert level during prescribed shooting exercises

Devices: None on medal (but see item 83)

---

83. Navy Rifle Marksmanship Ribbon

84. Navy Pistol Marksmanship Ribbon

Service: Navy

Criteria: Attainment of the minimum qualifying score during prescribed shooting exercises

Devices: Bronze, silver letter "E" (9, 10), bronze letter "S" (15)

---

85. Navy Distinguished Marksman Ribbon (obsolete)

86. Navy Distinguished Pistol Shot Ribbon (obsolete)

Service: Navy

Criteria: Attainment of the minimum qualifying score during prescribed shooting exercises

Devices: None

---

87. Navy Distinguished Marksman and Pistol Shot Ribbon (obsolete)

Service: Navy

Criteria: Attainment of the minimum qualifying score during prescribed shooting exercises

Devices: None

---

88. Small Arms Expert Marksmanship Ribbon

Service: Air Force

Instituted: 1962

Criteria: Qualification as expert with either the M-16 rifle or standard Air Force issue handgun

Devices: Bronze star (51)

88a. Small Arms Expert Marksmanship Ribbon

Service: Air Force

Shown with 3/16" diameter bronze star indicating additional weapon qualification

---

89. Coast Guard Expert Rifleman Medal

Service: Coast Guard

Criteria: Attainment of the minimum qualifying score for the expert level during prescribed shooting exercises

Devices: None on medal (but see item 91)

---

90. Coast Guard Expert Pistol Shot Medal

Service: Coast Guard

Criteria: Attainment of the minimum qualifying score for the expert level during prescribed shooting exercises

Devices: None on medal (but see item 92)

---

91. Coast Guard Rifle Marksmanship Ribbon

Service: Coast Guard

Criteria: Attainment of the minimum qualifying score during prescribed shooting exercises

Devices: Bronze, silver letter "E" (9, 10), silver letter "S" (16), bronze, silver rifle (40, 41), gold rifle target (77)

---

92. Coast Guard Pistol Marksmanship Ribbon

Service: Coast Guard

Criteria: Attainment of the minimum qualifying score during prescribed shooting exercises

Devices: Bronze, silver letter "E" (9, 10), silver letter "S" (16), bronze, silver pistol (38, 39), gold pistol target (76)

91a. Coast Guard Rifle Marksmanship Ribbon   **92a. Coast Guard Pistol Marksmanship Ribbon**

Shown With Applicable Ribbon Devices

1a. Silver Letter "S"		1b. Silver Letter "S"
2a. Silver Letter "E"	Bronze Letter "E" (obsolete)	2b. Silver Letter "E"
3a. Bronze Rifle		3b. Bronze Pistol
4a. Silver Rifle		4b. Silver Pistol
5a. Gold Rifle Target		5b. Gold Pistol Target

Note: The target device on ribbon 5a. above should be mounted on ribbon 5b. and vice versa.

Plate 6. Foreign Decorations & Non-U.S. Service Awards

93. French Croix de Guerre

94. Philippine Defense Medal

95. Philippine Liberation Medal

96. Philippine Independence Medal

97. RVN Gallantry Cross

98. Armed Forces Honor Medal

99. Staff Service Medal

100. Civil Actions Service Medal

101. RVN Campaign Medal

102. United Nations Service Medal (Korea)

103. United Nations Medal (Observer Medal)

104. Multinational Force and Observers Medal

105. Inter-American Defense Board Medal

106. Saudi Arabian Medal for the Liberation of Kuwait

107. Kuwaiti Medal for the Liberation of Kuwait

Foreign Decorations & Non-U.S. Service Awards

93. Croix de Guerre	94. Defense Medal/ Ribbon	95. Liberation Medal/ Ribbon	96. Independence Medal/Ribbon	97. Gallantry Cross
Country: France Instituted: 1941 Criteria: Individual feats of arms as recognized by mention in dispatches Devices: Bronze palm similar to (36), bronze, silver, gold stars similar to (73) through (75) denote level of award and additional awards Notes: Belgium awarded their own Croix de Guerre to selected U.S. personnel	Country: Republic of the Philippines Instituted: 1945 (Army: 1948) Criteria: Service in defense of the Philippines between 8 December 1941 and 15 June 1942 Devices: Bronze star (47) Notes: Only the ribbon may be worn on the U.S. military uniform	Country: Republic of the Philippines Instituted: 1945 (Army: 1948) Criteria: Service in the liberation of the Philippines between 17 October 1944 and 3 September 1945 Devices: Bronze star (47) Notes: Only the ribbon may be worn on the U.S. military uniform	Country: Republic of the Philippines Instituted: 1946 (Army: 1948) Criteria: Receipt of both the Philippine Defense and Liberation Medals/Ribbons. Originally presented to those present for duty in the Philippines on 4 July 1946 Devices: None Notes: Only the ribbon may be worn on U.S. military uniform	Country: Republic of Vietnam Instituted: 1950 Criteria: Deeds of valor and acts of courage/heroism while fighting the enemy Devices: Bronze palm similar to (36), bronze, silver, gold stars similar to (73) through (75) denote level of award and additional awards (see pages 53 through 57 for further data on Gallantry Cross devices)
98. Armed Forces Honor Medal	**99. Staff Service Medal**	**100. Civil Actions Service Medal**	**101. Republic of Vietnam Campaign Medal**	**102. United Nations Service Medal (Korea)**
Country: Republic of Vietnam Instituted: 1953 Criteria: For outstanding contributions to the training and development of RVN Armed Forces Devices: None Notes: 1st Class for officers is shown; the 2nd Class medal is silver and ribbon has no yellow edge stripes	Country: Republic of Vietnam Instituted: 1964 Criteria: For outstanding initiative and devotion to their staff duties Devices: None Notes: 1st Class for officers is shown; the 2nd Class ribbon has blue edges (vice green)	Country: Republic of Vietnam Instituted: 1964 Criteria: For outstanding achievements in the field of civic actions Devices: None Notes: 1st Class for officers is shown; the 2nd Class ribbon has no center red stripes	Service: All Services Instituted: 1966 Criteria: 6 months service in the Republic of Vietnam between 1961 and 1973 or if wounded, captured or killed in action during the above period Devices: Silver date bar (3) Notes: Bar inscribed "1961- " is the only authorized version	Service: All Services Instituted: 1951 Criteria: Service on behalf of the United Nations in Korea between 27 June 1950 and 27 July 1954 Devices: None Notes: Above date denotes when award was authorized for wear by U.S. military personnel
103. United Nations Medal (Observer Medal)	**104. Multinational Force and Observers Medal**	**105. Inter-American Defense Board Medal**	**106. Saudi Arabian Medal for the Liberation of Kuwait**	**107. Kuwaiti Medal for the Liberation of Kuwait**
Service: All Services Instituted: 1964 Criteria: 6 months service with any of the following U.N. operations: UNTSO, UNOGIL, UNMOGIP or UNSFH Devices: Bronze star (49) is pending Notes: Above date denotes when award was authorized for wear by U.S. military personnel	Service: All Services Instituted: 1982 Criteria: 6 months service with the Multinational Force & Observers peacekeeping force in the Sinai Desert Devices: Bronze numeral (23) Notes: Above date denotes when award was authorized for wear by U.S. military personnel	Service: All Services Instituted: 1982 Criteria: Service with the Inter-American Defense Board for at least one (1) year Devices: Gold star (67) Notes: Above date denotes when award was authorized for wear by U.S. military personnel	Service: All Services Instituted: 1992 Criteria: Participation in, or support of, Operation Desert Storm (1990-91) Devices: Gold palm tree device (37) Notes: Support must have been performed in theater (e.g.: Persian Gulf, Red Sea, Iraq, Kuwait, Saudi Arabia, Gulf of Oman, etc.)	Service: All Services Instituted: 1995 Criteria: Participation in, or support of, Operations Desert Shield and/or Desert Storm (1991-92) Devices: None Notes: Above date denotes when award was authorized for wear by U.S. military personnel

Plate 7. U.S. Awards Having No Medal Awards ("Ribbons-Only")

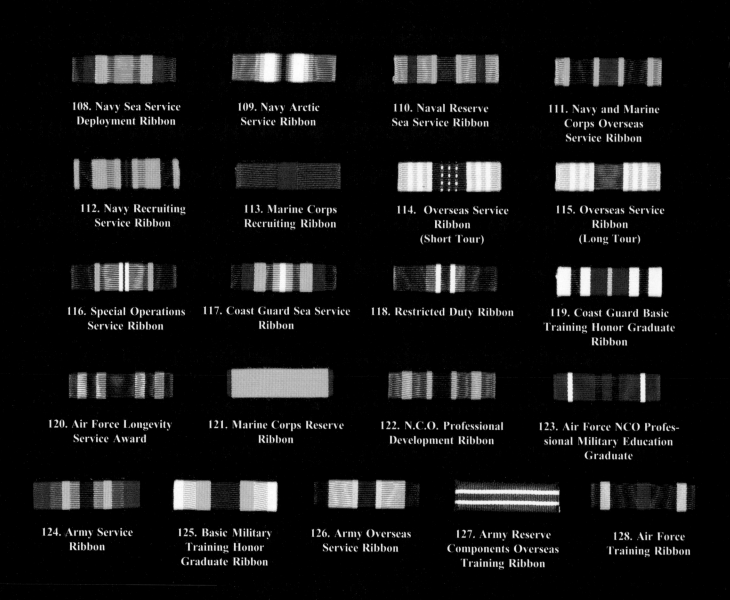

108. Navy Sea Service Deployment Ribbon

109. Navy Arctic Service Ribbon

110. Naval Reserve Sea Service Ribbon

111. Navy and Marine Corps Overseas Service Ribbon

112. Navy Recruiting Service Ribbon

113. Marine Corps Recruiting Ribbon

114. Overseas Service Ribbon (Short Tour)

115. Overseas Service Ribbon (Long Tour)

116. Special Operations Service Ribbon

117. Coast Guard Sea Service Ribbon

118. Restricted Duty Ribbon

119. Coast Guard Basic Training Honor Graduate Ribbon

120. Air Force Longevity Service Award

121. Marine Corps Reserve Ribbon

122. N.C.O. Professional Development Ribbon

123. Air Force NCO Professional Military Education Graduate

124. Army Service Ribbon

125. Basic Military Training Honor Graduate Ribbon

126. Army Overseas Service Ribbon

127. Army Reserve Components Overseas Training Ribbon

128. Air Force Training Ribbon

The ribbons described on this and the next few pages fall into a special class of honors known as "ribbon only" awards since there is no associated medal. Although the U.S. is not the only country which has employed this variety of award, it has certainly become the world's greatest proponent of the format.

The practice seems to stem from the late 19th century when various German states, among them Baden, Bavaria, Mecklenburg and Prussia, issued "schnalle" or buckles to members of their Landwehr (militia) as a reward for long and faithful service. The award usually consisted of a unicolored ribbon on which the sovereign's initials were embroidered along with other forms of ornamentation (e.g. Maltese crosses, the class of the award (II), etc.). The ribbon was surrounded by a metal frame and affixed to the uniform by a simple pin back, thus giving the impression of a belt buckle (hence the name).

The first U.S. ribbon only awards were the Presidential Unit

Citations established by the Army and Navy during World War II, both as a reward to units/ships cited for battle honors and to individuals who served in such units. As an interesting sidelight, all U.S. Army unit awards, by design or accident, reintroduce the buckle format by surrounding each ribbon with a gold frame containing a design of laurel leaves. The influence of the Senior Service may be seen in the unit awards issued by the Department of Defense and by our wartime allies (The Republics of the Philippines, Korea and Vietnam) all of which emulate the Army's gold frame arrangement.

The Marine Corps Reserve ribbon (now obsolete) was the first non-unit award to appear in this form and was the forerunner of a large number of ribbons having no medallic counterparts. Whether the form was selected due to simplicity, providing decorations and service medals a higher degree of stature or forced by budgetary considerations, it has certainly become a major element in the U.S. award structure. You may expect it to continue as a factor in future awards policies.

108. Navy Sea Service Deployment Ribbon Service: Navy/Marine Corps (Inst: 1981) Criteria: 12 months active duty on deployed vessels operating away from their home port for extended periods Devices: Bronze, silver star (52, 60)	**109. Navy Arctic Service Ribbon** Service: Navy/Marine Corps (Inst: 1986) Criteria: 28 days of service on naval vessels operating above the Arctic Circle Devices: None	**110. Naval Reserve Sea Service Ribbon** Service: Navy (Inst: 1986) Criteria: 24 months of cumulative service embarked on Naval Reserve vessels or an embarked Reserve unit Devices: Bronze, silver star (52, 60)	**111. Navy & Marine Corps Overseas Service Ribbon** Service: Navy/Marine Corps (Inst: 1986) Criteria: 12 months consecutive or accumulated duty at an overseas shore base duty station Devices: Bronze, silver star (52, 60)
112. Navy Recruiting Service Ribbon Service: Navy (Inst: 1989) Criteria: Successful completion of 3 consecutive years of recruiting duty Devices: Bronze, silver star (52, 60)	**113. Marine Corps Recruiting Ribbon** Service: Marine Corps (Inst: 1995- Retroactive to 1973) Criteria: Successful completion of 3 consecutive years of recruiting duty Devices: Bronze, silver star (52, 60)	**114. Overseas Service Ribbon (Short Tour)** Service: Air Force (Inst: 1980) Criteria: Successful completion of an overseas tour designated as "short term" by appropriate authority Devices: Bronze, silver oak leaf cluster (28, 32)	**115. Overseas Service Ribbon (Long Tour)** Service: Air Force (Inst: 1980) Criteria: Successful completion of an overseas tour designated as "long term" by appropriate authority Devices: Bronze, silver oak leaf cluster (28, 32)
116. Special Operations Service Ribbon Service: Coast Guard (Inst: 1987) Criteria: Participation in a Coast Guard special non-combat operation not recognized by another service award Devices: Bronze, silver star (55, 61)	**117. Coast Guard Sea Service Ribbon** Service: Coast Guard (Inst: 1984) Criteria: Satisfactory completion of a minimum of 12 months of cumulative sea duty Devices: Bronze, silver star (55, 61)	**118. Restricted Duty Ribbon** Service: Coast Guard (Inst: 1984) Criteria: Successful completion of a tour of duty at remote shore stations (LORAN stations, light ships, etc.) without family Devices: Bronze, silver star (55, 61)	**119. Coast Guard Basic Training Honor Graduate Ribbon** Service: Coast Guard (Inst: 1984) Criteria: Successful attainment of the top 3 percent of the class during Coast Guard recruit training Devices: None
120. Air Force Longevity Service Award Service: Air Force (Inst: 1957) Criteria: Successful completion of an aggregate total of four years of honorable active service Devices: Bronze, silver oak leaf cluster (28, 32)	**121. Marine Corps Reserve Ribbon** Service: Marine Corps (Inst: 1945) Criteria: Successful completion of 10 years of honorable service in any class of the Marine Corps Reserve Devices: Bronze star (52)	**122. N.C.O. Professional Development Ribbon** Service: Army (Inst: 1981) Criteria: Successful completion of designated NCO professional development courses Devices: Bronze numeral (24)	**123. N.C.O. Professional Military Education Graduate Ribbon** Service: Air Force (Inst: 1962) Criteria: Successful completion of a certified NCO professional military education school Devices: Bronze, silver oak leaf cluster (27, 31)

124. Army Service Ribbon Service: Army (Inst: 1981) Criteria: Successful completion of initial entry training Devices: None	**125. Basic Military Training Honor Graduate Ribbon** Service: Air Force (Inst: 1976) Criteria: Demonstration of excellence in all academic and military training phases of basic Air Force entry training Devices: None	**126. Army Overseas Service Ribbon** Service: Army (Inst: 1981) Criteria: Successful completion of normal overseas tours not recognized by any other service award Devices: Bronze numeral (25)	**127. Army Reserve Components Overseas Training Ribbon** Service: Army (Inst: 1984) Criteria: Successful completion of annual training or active duty training for 10 consecutive duty days on foreign soil Devices: Bronze numeral (25)	**128. Air Force Training Ribbon** Service: Air Force (Inst: 1980) Criteria: Successful completion of an Air Force accession training program Devices: Bronze, silver oak leaf cluster (27, 31)

Plate 8. U.S. and Foreign Unit Awards

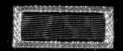

129. Army Presidential Unit Citation

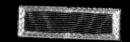

130. Navy Presidential Unit Citation

131. Air Force Presidential Unit Citation

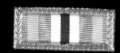

132. Joint Meritorious Unit Award

133. Army Valorous Unit Award

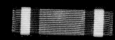

134. Navy Unit Commendation

135. Air Force Outstanding Unit Award

136. Dept. of Transportation Outstanding Unit Award

137. Coast Guard Unit Commendation

138. Army Meritorious Unit Commendaton

139. Navy Meritorious Unit Commendation

140. Air Force Organizational Excellence Award

141. Coast Guard Meritorious Unit Commendation

142. Coast Guard Meritorious Team Commendation

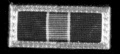

143. Army Superior Unit Award

144. Navy "E" Ribbon

145. Coast Guard "E" Ribbon

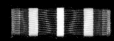

146. Coast Guard Bicentennial Unit Commendation

147. Philippine Presidential Unit Citation

148. Korean Presidential Unit Citation

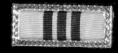

149. Vietnam Presidential Unit Citation

150. Republic of Vietnam Gallantry Cross Unit Citation

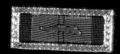

151. Republic of Vietnam Civil Actions Unit Citation

129. Army Presidential Unit Citation

Service: Army (Inst: 1942)

Criteria: Awarded to U.S. Army units for extraordinary heroism in action against an armed enemy

Devices: Bronze, silver oak leaf cluster (28, 32)
Notes: Original designation: Distinguished Unit Citation. Redesignated to present name in 1966

130. Navy Presidential Unit Citation

Service: Navy/Marine Corps/ Coast Guard (Inst: 1942)

Criteria: Awarded to Navy/ Marine Corps units for extraordinary heroism in action against an armed enemy

Devices: Gold globe (6), gold letter "N" (13), blue star (43), bronze, silver star (52, 60)

131. Air Force Presidential Unit Citation

Service: Air Force (Inst: 1957)

Criteria: Awarded to Air Force units for extraordinary heroism in action against an armed enemy

Devices: Bronze, silver oak leaf cluster (28, 32)
Notes: Original designation: Distinguished Unit Citation. Redesignated to present name in 1966

132. Joint Meritorious Unit Award

Service: All Services (Inst: 1982)

Criteria: Awarded to Joint Service units for meritorious achievement or service in combat or extreme circumstances

Devices: Army/Air Force/ Navy/Marine Corps: bronze, silver oak leaf cluster (29, 33); Coast Guard: bronze, silver star (56, 62)

133. Army Valorous Unit Award

Service: Army (Inst: 1963)

Criteria: Awarded to U.S. Army units for outstanding heroism in armed combat against an opposing armed force

Devices: Bronze, silver oak leaf cluster (28, 32)

134. Navy Unit Commendation

Service: Navy/Marine Corps (Inst: 1944)

Criteria: Awarded to units Navy/Marine Corps for outstanding heroism in action or extremely meritorious service

Devices: Bronze, silver star (52, 60)

135. Air Force Outstanding Unit Award

Service: Air Force (Inst: 1954)

Criteria: Awarded to U.S. Air Force units for exceptionally meritorious achievement or meritorious service

Devices: Bronze letter "V" (18), bronze, silver oak leaf cluster (28, 32)

136. Dept.of Transportation Outstanding Unit Award

Service: Coast Guard (Inst: 1994)

Criteria: Awarded to U.S. Coast Guard units for valorous or extremely meritorious service on behalf of the Transportation Dept.
Devices: Silver letter "O" (14), gold, silver star (64, 68)

137. Coast Guard Unit Commendation

Service: Coast Guard (Inst: 1963)

Criteria: Awarded to U.S. Coast Guard units for valorous or extremely meritorious service not involving combat

Devices: Silver letter "O" (14), gold, silver star (64, 68)

138. Army Meritorious Unit Commendation

Service: Army (Inst: 1944)

Criteria: Awarded to U.S. Army units for exceptionally meritorious conduct in the performance of outstanding service
Devices: Bronze, silver oak leaf cluster (28, 32)
Notes: Originally a golden wreath worn on the lower sleeve. Authorized in its present form in 1961

139. Navy Meritorious Unit Commendation

Service: Navy/Marine Corps (Inst: 1967)

Criteria: Awarded to Navy/ Marine Corps units for valorous actions or meritorious achievement (combat or noncombat)

Devices: Bronze, silver star (52, 60)

140. Air Force Organizational Excellence Award

Service: Air Force (Inst: 1969)

Criteria: Same as Outstanding Unit Award (see no.135 above) but awarded to unique unnumbered organizations performing staff functions

Devices: Bronze letter "V" (18), bronze, silver oak leaf cluster (28, 32)

141. Coast Guard Meritorious Unit Commendation

Service: Coast Guard (Inst: 1973)

Criteria: Awarded to U.S. Coast Guard units for valorous or meritorious achievement (combat or noncombat)
Devices: Silver letter "O" (14), gold, silver star (64, 68)

142. Coast Guard Meritorious Team Commendation

Service: Coast Guard (Inst: 1973)

Criteria: Awarded to smaller U.S. Coast Guard units for valorous or meritorious achievement (combat or noncombat)
Devices: Silver letter "O" (14), gold, silver star (64, 68)

143. Army Superior Unit Award

Service: Army (Inst: 1983)

Criteria: Awarded to U.S. Army units for meritorious performance in difficult and challenging peacetime missions

Devices: Bronze, silver oak leaf cluster (28, 32)

144. Navy "E" Ribbon

Service: Navy/Marine Corps (Inst: 1976)

Criteria: Awarded to ships or squadrons which have won battle efficiency competitions

Devices: Silver letter "E" (11), wreathed silver letter "E" (12)

145. Coast Guard "E" Ribbon

Service: Coast Guard (Inst: 1990)

Criteria: Awarded to U.S. Coast Guard ships and cutters which earn the overall operational readiness efficiency award

Devices: Gold, silver star (64, 68)

146. Coast Guard Bicentennial Unit Commendation

Service: Coast Guard (Inst: 1990)

Criteria: Awarded to all Coast Guard personnel serving satisfactorily at any time between 4 June 1989 and 4 June 1990
Devices: None

147. Philippine Presidential Unit Citation

Service: All Services (Inst: 1948)

Criteria: Awarded to units of the U.S. Armed Forces for service in the war against Japan and/or for 1970 and 1972 disaster relief
Devices: All Services (except Army) bronze star (45)

148. Korean Presidential Unit Citation

Service: All Services (Inst: 1951)

Criteria: Awarded to certain units of the U.S. Armed Forces for services rendered during the Korean War

Devices: None

149. Vietnam Presidential Unit Citation

Service: Army/Navy/Marine Corps/Coast Guard (Inst: 1954)

Criteria: Awarded to certain units of the U.S. Armed Forces for humanitarian service in the evacuation of civilians from North and Central Vietnam

Devices: None

150. Republic of Vietnam Gallantry Cross Unit Citation

Service: All Services (Inst: 1966)

Criteria: Awarded to certain units of the U.S. Armed Forces for valorous combat achievement during the Vietnam War, 1 March 1961 to 28 March 1974

Devices: Bronze palm, (34, 36), gold, silver, bronze star (73, 74, 75)

151. Republic of Vietnam Civil Actions Unit Citation

Service: All Services (Inst: 1966)

Criteria: Awarded to certain units of the U.S. Armed Forces for meritorious service during the Vietnam War, 1 March 1961 to 28 March 1974

Devices: Bronze palm (35)

Plate 9. Correct Manner of Wear- Ribbons of the U.S. Army

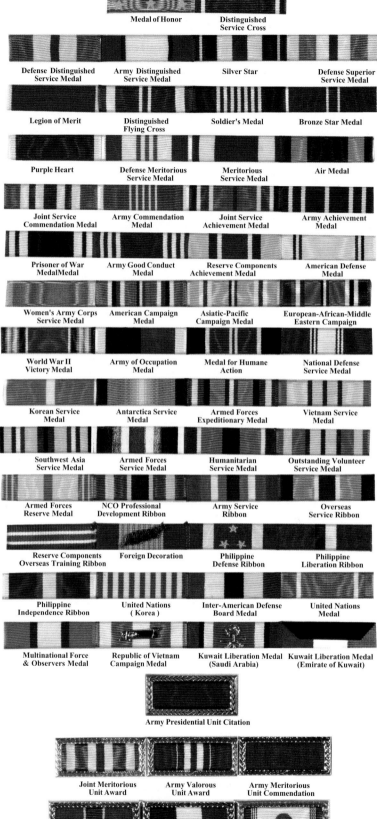

Medal of Honor

Distinguished Service Cross

Defense Distinguished Service Medal

Army Distinguished Service Medal

Silver Star

Defense Superior Service Medal

Legion of Merit

Distinguished Flying Cross

Soldier's Medal

Bronze Star Medal

Purple Heart

Defense Meritorious Service Medal

Meritorious Service Medal

Air Medal

Joint Service Commendation Medal

Army Commendation Medal

Joint Service Achievement Medal

Army Achievement Medal

Prisoner of War MedalMedal

Army Good Conduct Medal

Reserve Components Achievement Medal

American Defense Medal

Women's Army Corps Service Medal

American Campaign Medal

Asiatic-Pacific Campaign Medal

European-African-Middle Eastern Campaign

World War II Victory Medal

Army of Occupation Medal

Medal for Humane Action

National Defense Service Medal

Korean Service Medal

Antarctica Service Medal

Armed Forces Expeditionary Medal

Vietnam Service Medal

Southwest Asia Service Medal

Armed Forces Service Medal

Humanitarian Service Medal

Outstanding Volunteer Service Medal

Armed Forces Reserve Medal

NCO Professional Development Ribbon

Army Service Ribbon

Overseas Service Ribbon

Reserve Components Overseas Training Ribbon

Foreign Decoration

Philippine Defense Ribbon

Philippine Liberation Ribbon

Philippine Independence Ribbon

United Nations (Korea)

Inter-American Defense Board Medal

United Nations Medal

Multinational Force & Observers Medal

Republic of Vietnam Campaign Medal

Kuwait Liberation Medal (Saudi Arabia)

Kuwait Liberation Medal (Emirate of Kuwait)

UNIT AWARDS RIGHT BREAST

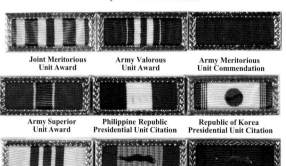

Army Presidential Unit Citation

Joint Meritorious Unit Award

Army Valorous Unit Award

Army Meritorious Unit Commendation

Army Superior Unit Award

Philippine Republic Presidential Unit Citation

Republic of Korea Presidential Unit Citation

Republic of Vietnam Presidential Unit Citation

Vietnam Gallantry Cross Unit Citation

Vietnam Civil Actions Unit Citation

38

U. S. Army Ribbon Devices

Left Breast

	Medal of Honor Bronze	**Distinguished Service Cross** Silver — Bronze	
Defense Distinguished Service Medal Bronze	**Army Distinguished Service Medal** Silver — Bronze	**Silver Star** Silver — Bronze	**Defense Superior Service Medal** Silver — Bronze
Legion of Merit Silver — Bronze	**Distinguished Flying Cross** Silver — Bronze	**Soldier's Medal** Bronze	**Bronze Star Medal** Bronze — Silver — Bronze
Purple Heart Silver — Bronze	**Defense Meritorious Service Medal** Silver — Bronze	**Meritorious Service Medal** Silver — Bronze	**Air Medal** Bronze — Bronze
Joint Service Commendation Medal Bronze — Silver — Bronze	**Army Commendation Medal** Bronze — Silver — Bronze	**Joint Service Achievement Medal** Silver — Bronze	**Army Achievement Medal** Silver — Bronze
Prisoner of War Medal Silver — Bronze	**Army Good Conduct Medal** Gold, Silver or Bronze Clasp	**Reserve Components Achievement Medal** Silver — Bronze	**American Defense Service Medal** Bronze
Women's Army Corps Service Medal None	**American Campaign Medal** Bronze	**Asiatic-Pacific Campaign Medal** Bronze — Silver — Bronze	**European-African-Middle Eastern Campaign** Bronze — Silver — Bronze
World War II Victory Medal None	**Army of Occupation Medal** Gold Airplane	**Medal for Humane Action** None	**National Defense Service Medal** Bronze
Korean Service Medal Bronze — Silver — Bronze	**Antarctica Service Medal** Bronze, Gold or Silver	**Armed Forces Expeditionary Medal** Bronze — Silver — Bronze	**Vietnam Service Medal** Bronze — Silver — Bronze
Southwest Asia Service Medal Bronze	**Armed Forces Service Medal** Silver — Bronze	**Humanitarian Service Medal** Silver — Bronze	**Outstanding Volunteer Service Medal** Bronze
Armed Forces Reserve Medal Bronze Hourglass — M Bronze	**NCO Professional Development Ribbon** Bronze	**Army Service Ribbon** None	**Overseas Service Ribbon** Bronze
Reserve Components Overseas Training Ribbon Bronze	**Foreign Decoration** As Specified by the Awarding Government	**Philippine Defense Ribbon** Bronze	**Philippine Liberation Ribbon** Bronze
Philippine Independence Ribbon None	**United Nations Service Medal** None	**Inter-American Defense Board Medal** Gold	**United Nations Medal** Bronze (Pending)
Multinational Force & Observers Medal Bronze	**Republic of Vietnam Campaign Medal** Silver Date Bar	**Kuwait Liberation Medal (Saudi Arabia)** Gold Palm Tree	**Kuwait Liberation Medal (Emirate of Kuwait)** None

Legend:
(complete information on attachments will be found on pages 52-57)

- = **Bronze Oak Leaf Cluster** Denotes second and subsequent awards of a decoration
- = **Silver Oak Leaf Cluster** Worn in lieu of five bronze oak leaf clusters
- ★ = **Bronze Service Star** Denotes second and subsequent awards of a service award or participation in a campaign or major operation
- ★ = **Silver Service Star** Worn in lieu of five bronze service stars
- V = **Bronze Letter "V"** Awarded for distinguished actions in combat
- ▲ = **Bronze Arrowhead** Denotes participation in parachute, glider or amphibious landing or assault
- M = **Letter "M"** Denotes reservists mobilized and called to active duty
- ◉ = **Antarctica Disk** Denotes personnel who "winter-over" on the Antarctic continent
- 3 = **Bronze Numeral** Denotes total number of awards of the Air Medal and certain service awards

Army Unit Awards

Right Breast

	Army Presidential Unit Citation Silver — Bronze	
Joint Meritorious Unit Award Silver — Bronze	**Army Valorous Unit Award** Silver — Bronze	**Army Meritorious Unit Commendation** Silver — Bronze
Army Superior Unit Award Silver — Bronze	**Philippine Republic Presidential Unit Citation** None	**Republic of Korea Presidential Unit Citation** None
Republic of Vietnam Presidential Unit Citation None	**Vietnam Gallantry Cross Unit Citation** Bronze Palm — Gold, Silver, Bronze	**Vietnam Civil Actions Unit Citation** Bronze Palm

39

**Plate 10.
Correct Manner
of Wear-
Ribbons of the
U.S. Navy**

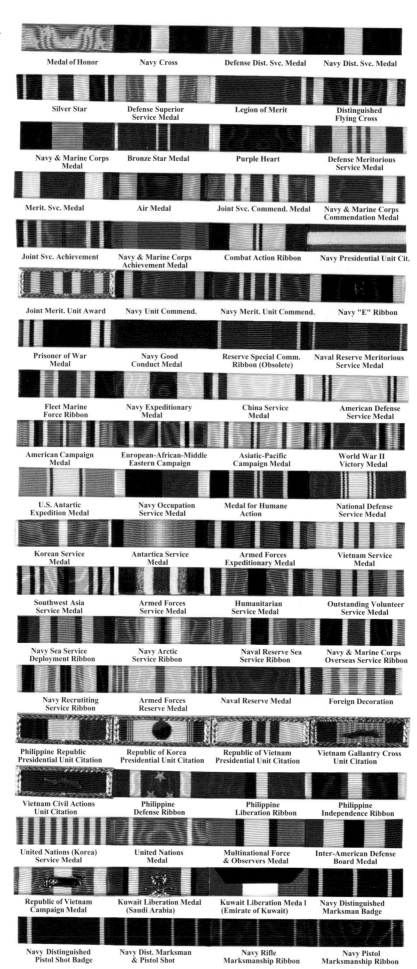

Medal of Honor Navy Cross Defense Dist. Svc. Medal Navy Dist. Svc. Medal

Silver Star Defense Superior Service Medal Legion of Merit Distinguished Flying Cross

Navy & Marine Corps Medal Bronze Star Medal Purple Heart Defense Meritorious Service Medal

Merit. Svc. Medal Air Medal Joint Svc. Commend. Medal Navy & Marine Corps Commendation Medal

Joint Svc. Achievement Navy & Marine Corps Achievement Medal Combat Action Ribbon Navy Presidential Unit Cit.

Joint Merit. Unit Award Navy Unit Commend. Navy Merit. Unit Commend. Navy "E" Ribbon

Prisoner of War Medal Navy Good Conduct Medal Reserve Special Comm. Ribbon (Obsolete) Naval Reserve Meritorious Service Medal

Fleet Marine Force Ribbon Navy Expeditionary Medal China Service Medal American Defense Service Medal

American Campaign Medal European-African-Middle Eastern Campaign Asiatic-Pacific Campaign Medal World War II Victory Medal

U.S. Antartic Expedition Medal Navy Occupation Service Medal Medal for Humane Action National Defense Service Medal

Korean Service Medal Antartica Service Medal Armed Forces Expeditionary Medal Vietnam Service Medal

Southwest Asia Service Medal Armed Forces Service Medal Humanitarian Service Medal Outstanding Volunteer Service Medal

Navy Sea Service Deployment Ribbon Navy Arctic Service Ribbon Naval Reserve Sea Service Ribbon Navy & Marine Corps Overseas Service Ribbon

Navy Recrutiing Service Ribbon Armed Forces Reserve Medal Naval Reserve Medal Foreign Decoration

Philippine Republic Presidential Unit Citation Republic of Korea Presidential Unit Citation Republic of Vietnam Presidential Unit Citation Vietnam Gallantry Cross Unit Citation

Vietnam Civil Actions Unit Citation Philippine Defense Ribbon Philippine Liberation Ribbon Philippine Independence Ribbon

United Nations (Korea) Service Medal United Nations Medal Multinational Force & Observers Medal Inter-American Defense Board Medal

Republic of Vietnam Campaign Medal Kuwait Liberation Medal (Saudi Arabia) Kuwait Liberation Meda l (Emirate of Kuwait) Navy Distinguished Marksman Badge

Navy Distinguished Pistol Shot Badge Navy Dist. Marksman & Pistol Shot Navy Rifle Marksmanship Ribbon Navy Pistol Marksmanship Ribbon

SEE PAGE 50 FOR RIGHT BREAST DISPLAY ON FULL DRESS UNIFORM

U. S. Navy Ribbon Devices

(complete information on attachments will be found on pages 52-57)

Ribbon	Devices
Medal of Honor	Gold (star)
Navy Cross	Silver, Gold (stars)
Defense Distinguished Service Medal	Bronze (oak leaf)
Navy Distinguished Service Medal	Silver, Gold (stars)
Silver Star	Silver, Gold (stars)
Defense Superior Service Medal	Silver, Bronze (oak leaf)
Legion of Merit	Bronze V, Silver, Gold (stars)
Distinguished Flying Cross	Bronze V, Silver, Gold (stars)
Navy & Marine Corps Medal	Gold (star)
Bronze Star Medal	Bronze V, Silver, Gold (stars)
Purple Heart	Silver, Gold (stars)
Defense Meritorious Service Medal	Silver, Bronze (oak leaf)
Meritorious Service Medal	Silver, Gold (stars)
Air Medal	Bronze, V, Silver, Gold, 5 Bronze
Joint Service Commendation Medal	Bronze V, Silver, Bronze (oak leaf)
Navy & Marine Corps Commendation Medal	Bronze V, Silver, Gold
Joint Service Achievement Medal	Silver, Bronze (oak leaf)
Navy & Marine Corps Achievement Medal	Bronze V, Silver, Gold
Combat Action Ribbon	Silver, Gold (stars)
Navy Presidential Unit Citation	O Gold, N Gold, Silver, Bronze
Joint Meritorious Unit Award	Silver, Bronze (oak leaf)
Navy Unit Commendation	Silver, Bronze (stars)
Navy Meritorious Unit Commendation	Silver, Bronze (stars)
Navy "E" Ribbon	E Silver, E Silver
Prisoner of War Medal	Silver, Bronze (stars)
Navy Good Conduct Medal	Silver, Bronze (stars)
Reserve Special Commendation Ribbon (Obsolete)	None
Naval Reserve Meritorious Service Medal	Silver, Bronze (stars)
Fleet Marine Force Ribbon	None
Navy Expeditionary Medal	W, Silver, Silver, Bronze
China Service Medal	Bronze (star)
American Defense Service Medal	Bronze, A Bronze
American Campaign Medal	Bronze (star)
European-African-Middle Eastern Campaign	Bronze, Silver, Bronze
Asiatic-Pacific Campaign Medal	Bronze, Silver, Bronze
World War II Victory Medal	None
U. S. Antarctic Expedition Medal	None
Navy Occupation Service Medal	Gold Airplane
Medal for Humane Action	None
National Defense Service Medal	Bronze (star)
Korean Service Medal	Bronze, Silver, Bronze
Antarctica Service Medal	Bronze, Gold or Silver
Armed Forces Expeditionary Medal	Bronze, Silver, Bronze
Vietnam Service Medal	Bronze, Silver, Bronze
Southwest Asia Service Medal	Bronze, Bronze
Armed Forces Service Medal	Silver, Bronze (stars)
Humanitarian Service Medal	Silver, Bronze (stars)
Outstanding Volunteer Service Medal	Bronze (star)
Navy Sea Service Deployment Ribbon	Silver, Bronze (stars)
Navy Arctic Service Ribbon	None
Naval Reserve Sea Service Ribbon	Silver, Bronze (stars)
Navy & Marine Corps Overseas Service Ribbon	Silver, Bronze (stars)
Navy Recruiting Service Ribbon	Silver, Bronze (stars)
Armed Forces Reserve Medal	Bronze Hourglass, M Bronze
Naval Reserve Medal (Obsolete)	None
Foreign Decoration	As Specified by the Awarding Government
Philippine Republic Presidential Unit Citation	Bronze (star)
Republic of Korea Presidential Unit Citation	None
Republic of Vietnam Presidential Unit Citation	None
Vietnam Gallantry Cross Unit Citation	Bronze Palm
Vietnam Civil Actions Unit Citation	Bronze Palm
Philippine Defense Ribbon	Bronze (star)
Philippine Liberation Ribbon	Bronze (star)
Philippine Independence Ribbon	None
United Nations Service Medal	None
United Nations Medal	Bronze (Pending)
Multinational Force & Observers Medal	5 Bronze
Inter-American Defense Board Medal	Gold (star)
Republic of Vietnam Campaign Medal	Silver Date Bar
Kuwait Liberation Medal (Saudi Arabia)	Gold Palm Tree
Kuwait Liberation Medal (Emirate of Kuwait)	None
Navy Distinguished Marksman Badge	None
Navy Distinguished Pistol Shot Badge	None
Navy Distinguished Marksman & Pistol Shot Badge	None
Navy Rifle Marksmanship Ribbon	E Silver, S Bronze
Navy Pistol Marksmanship Ribbon	E Silver, S Bronze

Legend:

- (star) = **Gold Service Star** Denotes second and subsequent awards of a decoration
- (star) = **Bronze Service Star** Denotes second and subsequent awards of a service award or participation in a campaign or operation
- (star) = **Silver Service Star** Worn in lieu of five gold or bronze service stars
- (oak leaf) = **Bronze Oak Leaf Cluster** Denotes second and subsequent awards of a Joint Service award
- (oak leaf) = **Silver Oak Leaf Cluster** Worn in lieu of five bronze oak leaf clusters
- V = **Bronze Letter "V"** Awarded for distinguished actions in combat
- A = **Bronze Letter "A"** Denotes service with Atlantic Fleet prior to World War II
- M = **Bronze Letter "M"** Denotes reservists mobilized and called to active duty
- (disk) = **Antarctica Disk** Denotes personnel who "winter-over" on the Antarctic continent
- (device) = **Marine Corps Device** Denotes combat service with Marine Corps Units
- 5 = **Bronze Numeral** Denotes total number of strike/flight awards of the Air Medal and other medals

Marksmanship Devices

- S = Letter "S"
- E = Letter "E"

Note: Per Navy regulations, no row may contain more than three (3) ribbons. The above display is arranged solely to conserve space on the page

Plate 11. Correct Manner of Wear- Ribbons of the U.S. Marine Corps

Medal of Honor   Navy Cross   Defense Distinguished Svc.

Navy Distinguished Svc.   Silver Star   Defense Superior Svc.   Legion of Merit

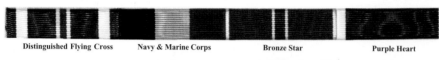

Distinguished Flying Cross   Navy & Marine Corps   Bronze Star   Purple Heart

Defense Meritorious Svc.   Meritorious Service   Air Medal   Joint Service Commend.

Navy & Marine Corps Comm.   Joint Svc. Achieve.   Navy & Marine Corps Achieve.   Combat Action

Navy Presidential Unit. Cit.   Joint Merit. Unit Award   Navy Unit Commend.   Navy Merit. Unit Commend.

Navy "E" Ribbon   Prisoner of War   Marine Corps Good Conduct   Selected Marine Corps Res.

Marine Corps Expeditionary   China Service   American Defense Svc.   American Campaign

European-African-Middle Eastern   Asiatic-Pacific   World War II Victory   Navy Occupation Svc.

Humane Action   National Defense Svc.   Korean Service   Antarctica Service

Armed Forces Expeditionary   Vietnam Service   Southwest Asia Svc.   Armed Forces Svc.

Humanitarian Service   Outstanding Volunteer Svc.   Navy Sea Svc. Deployment   Navy Arctic Svc.

Navy & Marine Corps Overseas Svc.   Marine Corps Recruit.   Armed Forces Res.   Marine Corps Reserve (obs.)

Foreign Decoration   Philippine Republic Presidential Unit Citation   Republic of Korea Presidential Unit Citation   Republic of Vietnam Presidential Unit Citation

Vietnam Gallantry Cross Unit Cit.   Vietnam Civil Actions Unit Cit.   Philippine Defense   Philippine Liberation

Philippine Indep. Ribbon   United Nations (Korea)   United Nations Medal   Multinat'l Force & Observers

Inter-American Defense Board   Republic of Vietnam Camp.   Kuwait Liberation Medal (Saudi Arabia)   Kuwait Liberation Medal (Emirate of Kuwait)

SEE PAGE 50 FOR RIGHT BREAST DISPLAY ON FULL DRESS UNIFORM

42

U. S. Marine Corps Ribbon Devices

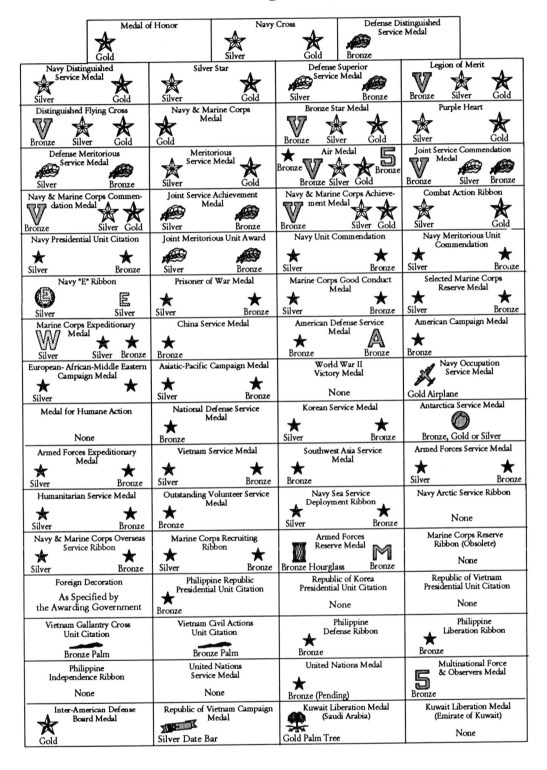

Legend:

(complete information on attachments will be found on pages 52-57)

★ = **Gold Service Star**
Denotes second and subsequent awards of a decoration

★ = **Bronze Service Star**
Denotes second and subsequent awards of a service award or participation in a campaign or major operation

★ = **Silver Service Star**
Worn in lieu of five gold or bronze service stars

🌿 = **Bronze Oak Leaf Cluster**
Denotes second and subsequent awards of a Joint Service decoration or unit citation

🌿 = **Silver Oak Leaf Cluster**
Worn in lieu of five bronze oak leaf clusters

V = **Bronze Letter "V"**
Awarded for distinguished actions in combat

W = **Letter "W"**
Denotes participation in Defense of Wake Island

M = **Bronze Letter "M"**
Denotes reservists mobilized and called to active duty

⬤ = **Antarctica Disk**
Denotes personnel who "winter-over" on the Antarctc continent

5 = **Bronze Numeral**
Denotes total number of strike/flight awards of the Air Medal and other awards

Plate 12.
Correct
Manner of
Wear-
Ribbons of
the U.S.
Air Force

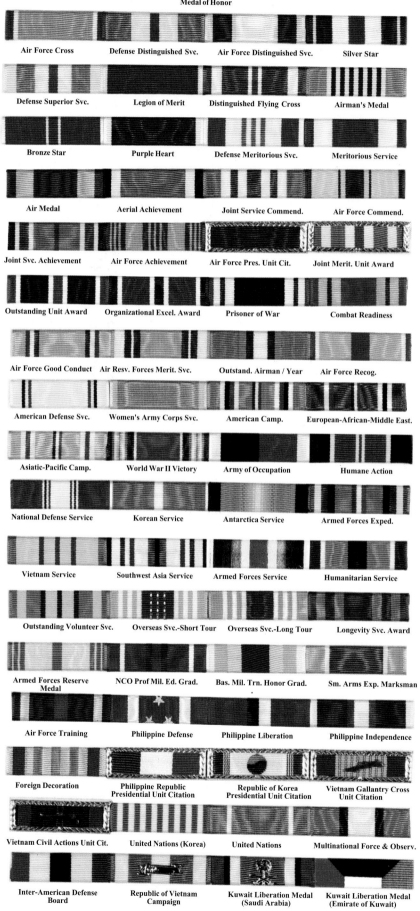

Medal of Honor

Air Force Cross | Defense Distinguished Svc. | Air Force Distinguished Svc. | Silver Star

Defense Superior Svc. | Legion of Merit | Distinguished Flying Cross | Airman's Medal

Bronze Star | Purple Heart | Defense Meritorious Svc. | Meritorious Service

Air Medal | Aerial Achievement | Joint Service Commend. | Air Force Commend.

Joint Svc. Achievement | Air Force Achievement | Air Force Pres. Unit Cit. | Joint Merit. Unit Award

Outstanding Unit Award | Organizational Excel. Award | Prisoner of War | Combat Readiness

Air Force Good Conduct | Air Resv. Forces Merit. Svc. | Outstand. Airman / Year | Air Force Recog.

American Defense Svc. | Women's Army Corps Svc. | American Camp. | European-African-Middle East.

Asiatic-Pacific Camp. | World War II Victory | Army of Occupation | Humane Action

National Defense Service | Korean Service | Antarctica Service | Armed Forces Exped.

Vietnam Service | Southwest Asia Service | Armed Forces Service | Humanitarian Service

Outstanding Volunteer Svc. | Overseas Svc.-Short Tour | Overseas Svc.-Long Tour | Longevity Svc. Award

Armed Forces Reserve Medal | NCO Prof Mil. Ed. Grad. | Bas. Mil. Trn. Honor Grad. | Sm. Arms Exp. Marksman

Air Force Training | Philippine Defense | Philippine Liberation | Philippine Independence

Foreign Decoration | Philippine Republic Presidential Unit Citation | Republic of Korea Presidential Unit Citation | Vietnam Gallantry Cross Unit Citation

Vietnam Civil Actions Unit Cit. | United Nations (Korea) | United Nations | Multinational Force & Observ.

Inter-American Defense Board | Republic of Vietnam Campaign | Kuwait Liberation Medal (Saudi Arabia) | Kuwait Liberation Medal (Emirate of Kuwait)

44

U. S. Air Force Ribbon Devices

	Medal of Honor		
	Bronze		

Air Force Cross	Defense Distinguished Service Medal	Air Force Distinguished Service Medal	Silver Star
Silver Bronze	Bronze	Silver Bronze	Silver Bronze
Defense Superior Service Medal	**Legion of Merit**	**Distinguished Flying Cross**	**Airman's Medal**
Silver Bronze	Silver Bronze	Silver Bronze	Bronze
Bronze Star Medal	**Purple Heart**	**Defense Meritorious Service Medal**	**Meritorious Service Medal**
Bronze Silver Bronze	Silver Bronze	Silver Bronze	Silver Bronze
Air Medal	**Aerial Achievement Medal**	**Joint Service Commendation Medal**	**Air Force Commendation Medal**
Silver Bronze	Silver Bronze	Bronze Silver Bronze	Silver Bronze
Joint Service Achievement Medal	**Air Force Achievement Medal**	**Air Force Presidential Unit Citation**	**Joint Meritorious Unit Award**
Silver Bronze	Silver Bronze	Silver Bronze	Silver Bronze
Outstanding Unit Award	**Organizational Excellence Award**	**Prisoner of War Medal**	**Combat Readiness Medal**
Bronze Silver Bronze	Bronze Silver Bronze	Silver Bronze	Silver Bronze
Air Force Good Conduct Medal	**Air Reserve Forces Meritorious Service Medal**	**Outstanding Airman of the Year Ribbon**	**Air Force Recognition Ribbon**
Silver Bronze	Silver Bronze	Bronze Silver Bronze	Silver Bronze
American Defense Service Medal	**Women's Army Corps Service Medal**	**American Campaign Medal**	**European-African-Middle Eastern Campaign**
Bronze	None	Bronze	Bronze Silver Bronze
Asiatic-Pacific Campaign Medal	**World War II Victory Medal**	**Army of Occupation Medal**	**Medal for Humane Action**
Bronze Silver Bronze	None	Gold Airplane	None
National Defense Service Medal	**Korean Service Medal**	**Antarctica Service Medal**	**Armed Forces Expeditionary Medal**
Bronze	Bronze Silver Bronze	Bronze, Gold or Silver	Silver Bronze
Vietnam Service Medal	**Southwest Asia Service Medal**	**Armed Forces Service Medal**	**Humanitarian Service Medal**
Silver Bronze	Bronze	Silver Bronze	Silver Bronze
Outstanding Volunteer Service Medal	**Overseas Service Ribbon-Short Tour**	**Overseas Service Ribbon-Long Tour**	**Longevity Service Award Ribbon**
Bronze	Silver Bronze	Silver Bronze	Silver Bronze
Armed Forces Reserve Medal	**NCO Professional Mil. Education Grad. Ribbon**	**Basic Military Training Honor Graduate Ribbon**	**Small Arms Expert Marksmanship Ribbon**
Bronze Hourglass Bronze (M)	Silver Bronze	None	Bronze
Air Force Training Ribbon	**Philippine Defense Ribbon**	**Philippine Liberation Ribbon**	**Philippine Independence Ribbon**
Silver Bronze	Bronze	Bronze	None
Foreign Decoration	**Philippine Republic Presidential Unit Citation**	**Republic of Korea Presidential Unit Citation**	**Vietnam Gallantry Cross Unit Citation**
As Specified by the Awarding Government	Bronze	None	Bronze Palm
Vietnam Civil Actions Unit Citation	**United Nations Service Medal**	**United Nations Medal**	**Multinational Force & Observers Medal**
Bronze Palm	None	Bronze (Pending)	Bronze Numeral
Inter-American Defense Board Medal	**Republic of Vietnam Campaign Medal**	**Kuwait Liberation Medal (Saudi Arabia)**	**Kuwait Liberation Medal (Emirate of Kuwait)**
Gold	Silver Date Bar	Gold Palm Tree	None

Legend:
(complete information on attachments will be found on pages 52-57)

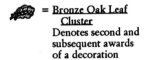

= **Bronze Oak Leaf Cluster**
Denotes second and subsequent awards of a decoration

= **Silver Oak Leaf Cluster**
Worn in lieu of five bronze oak leaf clusters

= **Bronze Service Star**
Denotes second and subsequent awards of a service award or participation in a campaign or major operation

= **Silver Service Star**
Worn in lieu of five bronze service stars

= **Bronze Letter "V"**
Awarded for distinguished actions in combat

= **Bronze Arrowhead**
Denotes participation in parachute, glider or amphibious landing or assault

= **Letter "M"**
Denotes reservists mobilized and called to active duty

= **Antarctica Disk**
Denotes personnel who "winter-over" on the Antarctic continent

Plate 13. Correct Manner of Wear- Ribbons of the U.S. Coast Guard

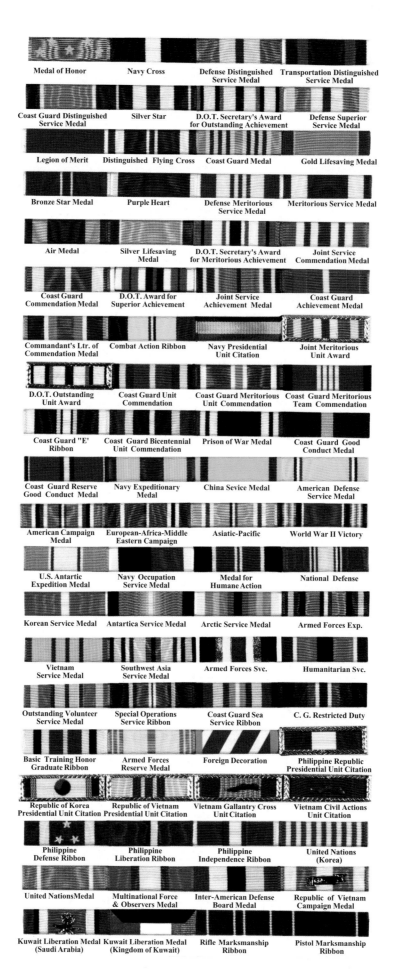

Medal of Honor | Navy Cross | Defense Distinguished Service Medal | Transportation Distinguished Service Medal

Coast Guard Distinguished Service Medal | Silver Star | D.O.T. Secretary's Award for Outstanding Achievement | Defense Superior Service Medal

Legion of Merit | Distinguished Flying Cross | Coast Guard Medal | Gold Lifesaving Medal

Bronze Star Medal | Purple Heart | Defense Meritorious Service Medal | Meritorious Service Medal

Air Medal | Silver Lifesaving Medal | D.O.T. Secretary's Award for Meritorious Achievement | Joint Service Commendation Medal

Coast Guard Commendation Medal | D.O.T. Award for Superior Achievement | Joint Service Achievement Medal | Coast Guard Achievement Medal

Commandant's Ltr. of Commendation Medal | Combat Action Ribbon | Navy Presidential Unit Citation | Joint Meritorious Unit Award

D.O.T. Outstanding Unit Award | Coast Guard Unit Commendation | Coast Guard Meritorious Unit Commendation | Coast Guard Meritorious Team Commendation

Coast Guard "E' Ribbon | Coast Guard Bicentennial Unit Commendation | Prison of War Medal | Coast Guard Good Conduct Medal

Coast Guard Reserve Good Conduct Medal | Navy Expeditionary Medal | China Sevice Medal | American Defense Service Medal

American Campaign Medal | European-Africa-Middle Eastern Campaign | Asiatic-Pacific | World War II Victory

U.S. Antartic Expedition Medal | Navy Occupation Service Medal | Medal for Humane Action | National Defense

Korean Service Medal | Antartica Service Medal | Arctic Service Medal | Armed Forces Exp.

Vietnam Service Medal | Southwest Asia Service Medal | Armed Forces Svc. | Humanitarian Svc.

Outstanding Volunteer Service Medal | Special Operations Service Ribbon | Coast Guard Sea Service Ribbon | C. G. Restricted Duty

Basic Training Honor Graduate Ribbon | Armed Forces Reserve Medal | Foreign Decoration | Philippine Republic Presidential Unit Citation

Republic of Korea Presidential Unit Citation | Republic of Vietnam Presidential Unit Citation | Vietnam Gallantry Cross Unit Citation | Vietnam Civil Actions Unit Citation

Philippine Defense Ribbon | Philippine Liberation Ribbon | Philippine Independence Ribbon | United Nations (Korea)

United NationsMedal | Multinational Force & Observers Medal | Inter-American Defense Board Medal | Republic of Vietnam Campaign Medal

Kuwait Liberation Medal (Saudi Arabia) | Kuwait Liberation Medal (Kingdom of Kuwait) | Rifle Marksmanship Ribbon | Pistol Marksmanship Ribbon

SEE PAGE 50 FOR RIGHT BREAST DISPLAY ON FULL DRESS UNIFORM

U. S. Coast Guard Ribbon Devices

Medal of Honor — Gold	**Navy Cross** — Silver / Gold	**Defense Distinguished Service Medal** — Gold	**Transportation Distinguished Service Medal** — Silver / Gold
Coast Guard Distinguished Service Medal — Gold	**Silver Star** — Silver / Gold	**D.O.T. Secretary's Award for Outstanding Achievement** — Gold	**Defense Superior Service Medal** — Silver / Gold
Legion of Merit — Bronze / Silver / Gold	**Distinguished Flying Cross** — Silver / Gold	**Coast Guard Medal** — Gold	**Gold Lifesaving Medal** — Gold
Bronze Star Medal — Bronze / Silver / Gold	**Purple Heart** — Silver / Gold	**Defense Meritorious Service Medal** — Silver / Gold	**Meritorious Service Medal** — Silver / Silver / Gold
Air Medal — Silver / Gold / Bronze (5)	**Silver Lifesaving Medal** — Gold	**D.O.T. Secretary's Award for Meritorious Achievement** — Gold	**Joint Service Commendation Medal** — Bronze / Silver / Gold
Coast Guard Commendation Medal — Bronze / Silver / Silver / Gold	**D.O.T. Award for Superior Achievement** — Gold	**Joint Service Achievement Medal** — Silver / Gold	**Coast Guard Achievement Medal** — Bronze / Silver / Silver / Gold
Commandant's Ltr. of Commendation Medal — Silver / Silver / Gold	**Combat Action Ribbon** — Silver / Gold	**Navy Presidential Unit Citation** — Silver / Bronze	**Joint Meritorious Unit Award** — Silver / Gold
D.O.T. Outstanding Unit Award — Gold	**Coast Guard Unit Commendation** — Silver / Silver / Gold	**C.G. Meritorious Unit Commendation** — Silver / Silver / Gold	**C.G. Meritorious Team Commendation** — Silver / Silver / Gold
Coast Guard "E" Ribbon — Silver / Gold	**Coast Guard Bicentennial Unit Commendation** — None	**Prisoner of War Medal** — Silver / Bronze	**Coast Guard Good Conduct Medal** — Silver / Bronze
Coast Guard Reserve Good Conduct Medal — Silver / Gold	**Navy Expeditionary Medal** — Silver / Bronze	**China Service Medal** — Bronze	**American Defense Service Medal** — Bronze / Bronze (A)
American Campaign Medal — Bronze	**European-African-Middle Eastern Campaign** — Silver / Bronze	**Asiatic-Pacific Campaign Medal** — Silver / Bronze	**World War II Victory Medal** — None
U. S. Antarctic Expedition Medal — None	**Navy Occupation Service Medal** — Gold Airplane	**Medal for Humane Action** — None	**National Defense Service Medal** — Bronze
Korean Service Medal — Silver / Bronze	**Antarctica Service Medal** — Bronze, Gold or Silver	**Arctic Service Medal** — Silver / Bronze	**Armed Forces Expeditionary Medal** — Silver / Bronze
Vietnam Service Medal — Silver / Bronze	**Southwest Asia Service Medal** — Bronze	**Armed Forces Service Medal** — Silver / Bronze	**Humanitarian Service Medal** — Silver / Bronze
Outstanding Volunteer Service Medal — Bronze	**Special Operations Service Ribbon** — Silver / Bronze	**Coast Guard Sea Service Ribbon** — Silver / Bronze	**Coast Guard Restricted Duty Ribbon** — Silver / Bronze
Basic Training Honor Graduate Ribbon — Silver / Bronze	**Armed Forces Reserve Medal** — Bronze Hourglass (M)	**Foreign Decoration** — As Specified by the Awarding Government	**Philippine Republic Presidential Unit Citation** — Bronze
Republic of Korea Presidential Unit Citation — None	**Republic of Vietnam Presidential Unit Citation** — None	**Vietnam Gallantry Cross Unit Citation** — Bronze Palm	**Vietnam Civil Actions Unit Citation** — Bronze Palm
Philippine Defense Ribbon — Bronze	**Philippine Liberation Ribbon** — Bronze	**Philippine Independence Ribbon** — None	**United Nations Service Medal** — None
United Nations Medal — Bronze (Pending)	**Multinational Force & Observers Medal** — Bronze	**Inter-American Defense Board Medal** — Gold	**Republic of Vietnam Campaign Medal** — Silver Date Bar
Kuwait Liberation Medal (Saudi Arabia) — Gold Palm Tree	**Kuwait Liberation Medal (Emirate of Kuwait)** — None	**Rifle Marksmanship Ribbon** — Silver / Silver, Bronze / Gold	**Pistol Marksmanship Ribbon** — Silver / Silver, Bronze / Gold

Legend:

(complete information on attachments will be found on pages 52-57)

- = **Gold Service Star** Denotes second and subsequent awards of a decoration or unit award
- = **Bronze Service Star** Denotes second and subsequent awards of a service award or participation in a campaign or major operation
- = **Silver Service Star** Worn in lieu of five bronze or silver service stars
- V = **Bronze Letter "V"** Awarded for distinguished actions in combat
- = **Operational Distinguishing Device** Denotes superior operational performance
- M = **Bronze Letter "M"** Denotes reservists mobilized and called to active duty
- = **Antarctica Disk** Denotes personnel who "winter-over" on the Antarctic continent
- A = **Bronze Letter "A"** Denotes service with Atlantic Fleet prior to World War II

Marksmanship Devices

- E = Letter "E"
- S = Letter "S"
- = M-14 Rifle
- = M1911A1 Pistol
- = Rifle Target
- = Pistol Target

Note: Per Coast Guard regulations, no row may contain more than three (3) ribbons. The above display is arranged solely to conserve space on the page

Plate 14. U.S. Merchant Marine Ribbons

**Correct Order
for U.S.
Merchant
Marine**

Merchant Marine Ribbon Devices

	Distinguished Service Medal None	
Meritorious Service Medal None	Mariner's Medal None	Gallant Ship Citation Bar 🌊 Silver
Merchant Marine Combat Bar ⭐ Silver	Prisoner of War Medal ★ Bronze	Merchant Marine Defense Medal None
Atlantic War Zone Medal None	Pacific War Zone Medal None	Mediterranean- Middle East War Zone Medal None
World War II Victory Medal None	Korean Service Medal None	Vietnam Service Medal None

Merchant Marine Expeditionary Medal ★ Bronze	Philippine Defense Ribbon ★ Bronze	Philippine Liberation Ribbon ★ Bronze	40th Anniversary of World War II (USSR) None

Note: Some references show the Mariner's Medal and the Gallant Ship Citation Bar reversed in precedence.

Legend:
(complete information on attachments will be found on pages 52-57)

⭐ = <u>Silver Service Star</u>
Indicates crew member forced to abandon ship

★ = <u>Bronze Service Star</u>
Denotes second and subsequent awards of a service award or participation in a campaign or operation

🌊 = <u>Silver Seahorse</u>
Worn in Gallant Ship Citation Bar upon initial issue but has no significance

U.S. MERCHANT MARINE MEDALS AND DECORATIONS

To you who answered the call of your country and served in its Merchant Marine ... President Harry S. Truman

Gallant Ship Plaque

Distinguished Service Medal
The Merchant Marine's Highest Award

Under authority of Public law 100-324, the Maritime Administration shall award this medal to seamen who distinguished themselves by outstanding conduct or service beyond the line of duty

Meritorious Service Medal

Under authority of Public Law 100-324, the Maritime Administration shall award this medal to seamen for conduct or service of a meritorious nature.

Gallant Ship Citation Ribbon

Awarded to officers and seamen who served on a ship which, at the time of service, was cited for gallantry by the Maritime Administration. The bronze plaque is awarded to the ship.

Mariner's Medal
(World War II)

Awarded to a seaman who, while serving on a ship from December 7, 1941, and July 25, 1947, was wounded or suffered physical injury as a result of an act of an enemy of the United States.

Merchant Marine Defense Medal
(World War II)

Awarded for service in the U.S. Merchant Marine prior to Pearl Harbor. It may be worn by all merchant seamen who served as members of the crews of U.S. merchant ships from September 8, 1939, and December 7, 1941.

Atlantic War Zone Medal
(World War II)

Awarded for service in the Atlantic War Zone, including the North Atlantic, South Atlantic, Gulf of Mexico, Carribean, Barents Sea, and the Greenland Sea, during the period December 7, 1941, to November 8, 1945.

Mediterranean-Middle East War Zone Medal
(World War II)

Awarded for service in the zone including the Mediterranean Sea, Red Sea, Arabian Sea, and Indian Ocean west of 80 degrees east longitude, during the period December 7, 1941, to November 8, 1945.

Pacific War Zone Medal
(World War II)

Awarded for service in the Pacific War Zone, including the North Pacific, South Pacific, and the Indian Ocean east of 80 degrees east longitude, during the period December 7, 1941, to March 2, 1946.

Merchant Marine Combat Bar
(World War II)

Awarded to merchant seamen who served on a ship which at the same time of such service was attacked or damaged by an instrumentality of war from December 7, 1941, and July 25, 1947. A star is attached if the seaman was forced to abandon ship. For each additional abandonment a star is added.

Merchant Marine Emblem
(World War II)

The emblem is an identifying insigne that was issued to active merchant seamen for service from December 7, 1941, to July 25, 1947.

Victory Medal
(World War II)

Awarded to members of the crews of ships who served for 30 days or more during the period December 7, 1941, to September 3, 1945.

Honorable Service Button
(World War II)

Awarded to members of the crews of ships who served for 30 days during the period December 7, 1941, to September 3, 1945.

DEPARTMENT OF DEFENSE AND FOREIGN GOVERNMENTS RECOGNITION

Prisoner of War Medal
(U.S. Department of Defense)

Awarded to World War II merchant marine veterans held prisoners of war during the period December 7, 1941, to August 15, 1945. The medal recognizes the special service prisoners of war gave to their country and the suffering and anguish they endured while incarcerated.

Soviet Commemorative Medal

Awarded to merchant marine veterans who participated in convoys to Murmansk during World War II.

Phillippine Defense Ribbon

Awarded to members of crews of ships who served in Philippine waters for not less than 30 days from December 8, 1941, to June 15, 1942.

Phillippine Liberation Ribbon

Awarded to members of crews of ships who served in Philippine waters for not less than 30 days from October 17, 1944, to September 3, 1945.

Korean Service Medal

Awarded for service in the merchant marine from June 30, 1950, and September 30, 1953 in waters adjacent to Korea.

Vietnam Service Medal

Awarded for service in the merchant marine from July 4, 1965, and August 15, 1973 in waters adjacent to Vietnam.

Merchant Marine Expeditionary Award

Awarded to American merchant seamen who serve on U.S.-flag ships in support of operations involving American and allied military forces, as authorized by the Maritime Administration.

U.S. Department of Transportation

Maritime Administration

Applications for or inquiries relating to merchant marine medals and decorations should be directed to U.S. Department of Transportation, Maritime Administration, Office of Maritime Labor and Training, Washington, DC 20590.

9. RIGHT BREAST DISPLAYS/FULL DRESS

The three Naval Services prescribe the wear of "ribbon-only" awards on the <u>right</u> breast of the full dress uniform when large medals are worn. The required displays are as follows:

NAVY

	Navy Presidential Unit Citation	Combat Action Ribbon
Navy Meritorious Unit Commendation	Navy Unit Commendation	Joint Meritorious Unit Award
Fleet Marine Force Ribbon	Reserve Special Commendation Ribbon	Navy "E" Ribbon
Naval Reserve Sea Service Ribbon	Arctic Service Ribbon	Sea Service Deployment Ribbon
Philippine President-ial Unit Citation	Navy Recruiting Service Ribbon	Navy & M/Corps Over-seas Service Ribbon
Vietnam Gallantry Cross Unit Citation	Vietnam Presidential Unit Citation	Korean Presidential Unit Citation
Philippine Liberation Ribbon	Philippine Defense Ribbon	Vietnam Civil Actions Unit Citation
Pistol Marksmanship Ribbon	Rifle Marksmanship Ribbon	Philippine Independence Ribbon

MARINE CORPS

	Combat Action Ribbon	
Navy Presidential Unit Citation	Joint Meritorious Unit Award	Navy Unit Commendation
Navy Meritorious Unit Commendation	Navy "E" Ribbon	Sea Service Deployment Ribbon
Arctic Service Ribbon	Navy & M/Corps Over-seas Service Ribbon	Marine Corps Recruiting Ribbon
Marine Corps Reserve Ribbon	Philippine President-ial Unit Citation	Korean Presidential Unit Citation
Vietnam Presidential Unit Citation	Vietnam Gallantry Cross Unit Citation	Vietnam Civil Actions Unit Citation
Philippine Defense Ribbon	Philippine Liberation Ribbon	Philippine Independence Ribbon

COAST GUARD

Navy Presidential Unit Citation	Combat Action Ribbon	Commandant's Letter of Commendation Ribbon
Coast Guard Unit Commendation	D.O.T. Outstanding Unit Award	Joint Meritorious Unit Award
Coast Guard "E" Ribbon	C.G. Meritorious Team Commendation	C.G. Meritorious Unit Commendation
Coast Guard Sea Service Ribbon	Special Operations Service Ribbon	C.G. Bicentennial Unit Commendation
Philippine President-ial Unit Citation	Basic Training Honor Graduate Ribbon	Restricted Duty Ribbon
Vietnam Gallantry Cross Unit Citation	Vietnam Presidential Unit Citation	Korean Presidential Unit Citation
Philippine Liberation Ribbon	Philippine Defense Ribbon	Vietnam Civil Actions Unit Citation
Pistol Marksmanship Ribbon	Rifle Marksmanship Ribbon	Philippine Independence Ribbon

10. ATTACHMENTS and DEVICES

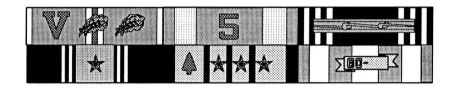

Looking back from the perspective of the late 20th century, it is apparent that early in the history of the U.S. awards program, little attention was paid to the possibility that a medal could be bestowed upon an individual more than once. This was to cause some embarrassment when five individuals (three Army and two Marine Corps) won second awards of the Medal of Honor in the span of years between the Civil War and World War I.

In contrast, the British Empire had recognized this need as far back as 1856 when the Victoria Cross was instituted. The original Royal Warrant authorized the use of an ornate bar affixed to the medal's suspension ribbon to represent the second award of the Cross. The bar, however, was not used universally and had to be authorized on an individual basis as each new medal was introduced for many years thereafter. Also to be noted, the custom of wearing a device directly on the ribbon bar to denote an additional award was still many years away, not finding its way into Victoria Cross regulations until 1916.

Although no one in possession of all his faculties would characterize World War I as an Age of Enlightenment, that certainly describes the era from the standpoint of medal and ribbon devices. By the end of the Great War, the use of ribbon attachments was quite widespread throughout the world and the U.S. had instituted its first four ribbon attachments, thus setting the stage for the many such accessories which would follow.

The best known of these, the oak leaf cluster, was established (although not by that name) at the same time that the Army's Distinguished Service Cross and Distinguished Service Medal came into being. The 1918 regulations provided for "..a bar or other suitable device.." for each succeeding deed or act sufficient to justify a subsequent award".

The same act authorized the use of a silver star device, three-sixteenths of an inch in diameter to denote a citation for gallantry in action. Although the directive seemed quite straightforward, it never made clear the actual ribbon to which the star should be affixed. However, the War Department directed that it be used on the appropriate service medal/ribbon. This led to a large number of retroactive awards, some dating back to the Civil War, but of greater significance, to the establishment of the Silver Star Medal as described earlier in this book. As a footnote to this discussion, the U.S. Navy also adopted the small silver star device but only for wear on the ribbon of the World War I Victory Medal after the receipt of a letter of commendation for performance of duty not justifying the award of the Medal of Honor, Navy Cross or Distinguished Service Medal (the only decorations in existence at the time).

For the record, the other two ribbon attachments authorized for use just after the Great War were the 3/16" diameter bronze stars representing the battle clasps to the Victory Medal and the bronze scroll numeral (now obsolete) used on the Marine Corps Expeditionary Ribbon (not a Medal yet!) to indicate the number of additional awards of the ribbon. Note that the Navy did not authorize its 5/16" diameter gold star to denote additional awards of a decoration until the early 1920s.

The great number of decorations and awards created during World War II also resulted in a vast increase in the number of available devices. The most significant of these was the silver device used in a five-for-one swap to eliminate the clutter that resulted from the huge number of decorations being awarded at the time. As an example, an Airman could now display 13 awards of the Air Medal with only four oak leaf clusters, 2 bronze and 2 silver, with the ribbon itself representing one award. The Navy's 5/16" silver star and the universally-used 3/16" silver "battle star" also aided in the war on ribbon clutter.

This is not to say that the device situation today is as clear as crystal. The bare fact is that, exclusive of the Merchant Marine, only 9 ribbons authorized since World War II have **no** device associated with their wear on the uniform. More to the point, there are only four ribbons awarded today that fit this category.

The large number of devices employed on the modern ribbon chest might seem excessive but, given the use of awards as a means of managing today's vastly scaled-down military establishment, it makes some sense. One need only examine the awards of the former Soviet Union to witness the results of having NO means to represent multiple awards of a medal. The great World War II military leaders, in wearing every medal they possessed, virtually covered every available square inch of their tunics with gongs.

Thus, to make some sense of the American system of devices and attachments, the reader is invited to examine the illustrations and tables on the next six pages, noting that the reference number under each device and in the left-hand column of the table is keyed to the earlier text material describing each associated award.

Plate 16- Attachments/Devices Used on American Ribbons- Sheet 1

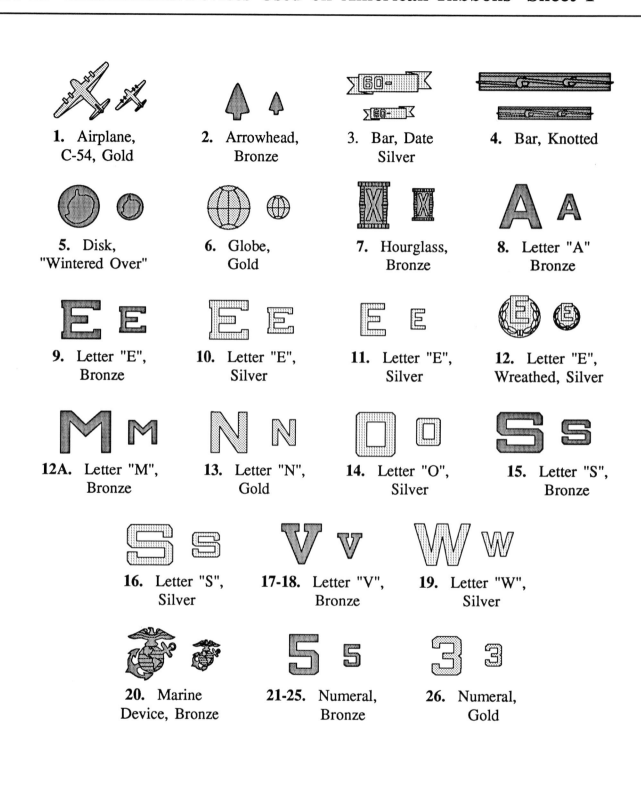

1. Airplane, C-54, Gold

2. Arrowhead, Bronze

3. Bar, Date Silver

4. Bar, Knotted

5. Disk, "Wintered Over"

6. Globe, Gold

7. Hourglass, Bronze

8. Letter "A" Bronze

9. Letter "E", Bronze

10. Letter "E", Silver

11. Letter "E", Silver

12. Letter "E", Wreathed, Silver

12A. Letter "M", Bronze

13. Letter "N", Gold

14. Letter "O", Silver

15. Letter "S", Bronze

16. Letter "S", Silver

17-18. Letter "V", Bronze

19. Letter "W", Silver

20. Marine Device, Bronze

21-25. Numeral, Bronze

26. Numeral, Gold

Note: All devices are shown both actual size and slightly larger than normal to enhance device details

52

Plate 16- Attachments/Devices Used on American Ribbons- Sheet 2

27-30. Oak Leaf Cluster, Bronze

31-33. Oak Leaf Cluster, Silver

34-35. Palm, Bronze

36. Palm, Bronze

37. Palm Tree & Swords, Gold

38. Pistol, M1911A1, Bronze

39. Pistol, M1911A1, Silver

40. Rifle, M14, Bronze

41. Rifle, M14, Silver

42. Seahorse, Silver

43. Star, 3/16", Blue

44-57. Star, 3/16", Bronze

58-63. Star, 3/16", Silver

64-67. Star, 5/16", Gold

68-72. Star, 5/16", Silver

73. Star, 3/8", Bronze

74. Star, 3/8", Gold

75. Star, 3/8", Silver

76. Target, Pistol, Gold

77. Target Rifle, Gold

Note: All devices are shown both actual size and slightly larger than normal to enhance device details

ATTACHMENTS/DEVICES USED ON AMERICAN RIBBONS

NO	DEVICE	RIBBON USE	DENOTES
1	Airplane, C-54 Gold	ALL SERVICES- World War II Occupation Medal	Berlin Airlift participation
2	Arrowhead, Bronze	ARMY and AIR FORCE- Campaign awards since World War II	Participation in combat glider landing, combat parachute jump or amphibious assault landing
3	Bar, Date, Silver	ALL SERVICES- Republic of Vietnam Campaign Medal	No significance- worn upon initial issue
4	Bar, Knotted: Bronze. . . . . Silver. . . . . Gold	ARMY- Good Conduct Medal	Additional awards: Nos. 2 - 5 Nos. 6 - 10 Nos. 11 - 15
5	Disk, "Wintered-Over" Bronze. . . . . Gold . . . . Silver.	ALL SERVICES- Antarctica Service Medal	Wintering over on the Antarctic Continent: 1 winter 2 winters 3 winters
6	Globe, Gold	NAVY- Presidential Unit Citation	Service aboard USS Triton during 1st submerged cruise around the world
7	Hourglass, Bronze	ALL SERVICES: Armed Forces Reserve Medal	Additional award
8	Letter "A", Bronze	NAVY, MARINE CORPS, COAST GUARD- American Defense Service Medal	Atlantic Fleet service prior to World War II
9	Letter "E", Bronze	NAVY and COAST GUARD- Marksmanship awards	Expert- 1st qualification (obsolete)
10	Letter "E", Silver	NAVY and COAST GUARD- Marksmanship awards	Expert qualification
11	" " "	NAVY and MARINE CORPS Navy "E" Ribbon	One (1) device per award- three (3) maximum
12	Letter "E", Silver, Wreathed	NAVY and MARINE CORPS Navy "E" Ribbon	4th (final) award
12A	Letter "M", Bronze	ALL SERVICES- Armed Forces Reserve Medal	Mobilization Device for Reservists called to active duty
13	Letter "N", Gold	NAVY- Presidential Unit Citation	Service aboard USS Nautilus during first cruise under the north polar ice cap
14	Letter "O", Silver	COAST GUARD- Decorations and unit awards	Operational Distinguishing Device
15	Letter "S", Bronze	NAVY- Marksmanship awards	Sharpshooter qualification
16	Letter "S", Silver	COAST GUARD- Marksmanship awards	Sharpshooter qualification

ATTACHMENTS/DEVICES USED ON AMERICAN RIBBONS

NO	DEVICE	RIBBON USE	DENOTES
17	Letter "V", Bronze	ALL SERVICES- Decorations	Combat Distinguishing Device
18	Letter "V", Bronze	AIR FORCE- Unit awards	Combat Distinguishing Device
19	Letter "W", Silver	NAVY and MARINE CORPS- Expeditionary Medals	Participation in defense of Wake Island- (1941)
20	Marine Corps Device, Bronze	NAVY and COAST GUARD- Campaign awards since World War II	Combat service by Naval personnel with Marine Corps units
21	Numeral, Block, Bronze	NAVY and MARINE CORPS	Total number of strike/flight awards
22	" " "	ALL SERVICES (except COAST GUARD)- Humanitarian Service Medal	Additional awards (obsolete)
23	" " "	ALL SERVICES- Multinational Force and Observer's Medal	Total number of awards
24	" " "	ARMY- NCO Professional Development Ribbon	Level of professional training attained:

Basic Ribbon. . . . . .Primary Level
Numeral "2". . . . . .Basic Level
Numeral "3". . . . . .Advanced Level
Numeral "4". . . . . .Senior Level
Numeral "5" (obsolete) . . . . .Sergeants Major Academy

NO	DEVICE	RIBBON USE	DENOTES
25	" " "	AIR FORCE- Air Medal and service awards	Total awards of awards
26	Numeral, Block, Gold	NAVY and MARINE CORPS- Air Medal	Number of individual awards (obsolete)
27	Oak Leaf Cluster, Bronze	AIR FORCE- Achievement awards	Additional awards
28	" " "	ARMY and AIR FORCE- Decorations, service and unit awards	Additional awards
29	" " "	ALL SERVICES- (except COAST GUARD)- Joint Service decorations and Joint Meritorious Unit Award	Additional awards
30	" " "	ARMY- National Defense Service Medal	Additional award (obsolete)
31	Oak Leaf Cluster, Silver	AIR FORCE- Achievement awards	5 additional awards
32	" " "	ARMY and AIR FORCE- Decorations, service and unit awards	5 additional awards
33	" " "	ALL SERVICES- (except COAST GUARD)- Joint Service decorations and Joint Meritorious Unit Award	5 additional awards
34	Palm, Bronze	ALL SERVICES- (except ARMY) Republic of Vietnam Gallantry Cross Unit Citation	No significance- worn upon initial issue

ATTACHMENTS/DEVICES USED ON AMERICAN RIBBONS

NO	DEVICE	RIBBON USE	DENOTES
35	Palm, Bronze	ARMY- Republic of Vietnam Gallantry Cross Unit Citation	Level of award ("cited before the Army") and additional awards
36	Palm, Bronze (cont'd)	ALL SERVICES- Republic of Vietnam Civil Actions Unit Citation	No significance- worn upon initial issue
37	Palm Tree with Swords, Gold	ALL SERVICES- Kuwait Liberation Medal (Saudi Arabia)	No significance- worn upon initial issue
38	Pistol, M1911A1, Bronze	COAST GUARD- Pistol Marksmanship Ribbon	Recipient of Pistol Shot Excellence in Competition Badge (Bronze)
39	Pistol, M1911A1, Silver	COAST GUARD- Pistol Marksmanship Ribbon	Recipient of Pistol Shot Excellence in Competition Badge (Silver)
40	Rifle, M14, Bronze	COAST GUARD- Rifle Marksmanship Ribbon	Recipient of Rifleman Excellence in Competition Badge (Bronze)
41	Rifle, M14, Silver	COAST GUARD- Rifle Marksmanship Ribbon	Recipient of Rifleman Excellence in Competition Badge (Silver)
42	Seahorse, Silver	MERCHANT MARINE- Gallant Ship Citation Bar	No significance- worn upon initial issue
43	Star, 3/16", Blue	NAVY- Presidential Unit Citation	Additional awards (obsolete)
44	Star, 3/16", Bronze	ALL SERVICES- National Defense Service Medal	Additional awards
45	" " "	ALL SERVICES- (except ARMY)- Philippine Republic Presidential Unit Citation	Additional award
46	" " "	ALL SERVICES- Campaign awards since World War II	Major battle participation (one star per major engagement)
47	" " "	ALL SERVICES- Philippine Defense and Liberation Ribbons	Additional battle honors
48	" " "	ALL SERVICES- American Defense Service Medal	Foreign service prior to World War II
49	" " "	ALL SERVICES- Service awards	Additional awards
50	" " "	AIR FORCE- Outstanding Airman of the Year Ribbon	"One of 12" competition finalist
51	" " "	AIR FORCE- Small Arms Expert Marksmanship Ribbon	Additional weapon qualification
52	" " "	NAVY and MARINE CORPS- Unit and service awards	Additional awards
53	" " "	NAVY and MARINE CORPS- Air Medal	First individual award
54	" " "	NAVY, MARINE CORPS and COAST GUARD- China Service Medal	Additional award (extended service)
55	" " "	COAST GUARD- Service awards	Additional awards

ATTACHMENTS/DEVICES USED ON AMERICAN RIBBONS

NO	DEVICE	RIBBON USE	DENOTES
56	Star, 3/16", Bronze (cont'd)	COAST GUARD- Joint Meritorious Unit Award	Additional award
57	" " "	MERCHANT MARINE- Expeditionary Medal	Additional awards
58	Star, 3/16", Silver	ALL SERVICES- Campaign awards since World War II	Participation in 5 major battles/campaigns
59	" " "	ALL SERVICES- Service awards	5 additional awards
60	" " "	NAVY and MARINE CORPS- Unit and service awards	5 additional awards
61	" " "	COAST GUARD- Service awards	5 additional awards
62	" " "	COAST GUARD- Joint Meritorious Unit Award	5 additional awards
63	" " "	MERCHANT MARINE- Combat Bar	Crew member forced to abandon ship (1 star per sinking)
64	Star, 5/16", Gold	COAST GUARD- Unit awards	Additional awards
65	" " "	COAST GUARD- Joint Service decorations	Additional awards
66	" " "	NAVY, MARINE CORPS and COAST GUARD- Decorations	Additional awards
67	" " "	ALL SERVICES- Inter-American Defense Board Medal	Additional awards
68	Star, 5/16", Silver	COAST GUARD- Unit awards	5 additional awards
69	" " "	COAST GUARD- Joint Service decorations	5 additional awards
70	" " "	NAVY, MARINE CORPS and COAST GUARD- Decorations	5 additional awards
71	" " "	NAVY and MARINE CORPS- Unit awards	5 additional awards (obsolete)
72	" " "	NAVY and MARINE CORPS- Campaign awards	Participation in 5 major battles (obsolete)
73	Star, 3/8", Bronze	ARMY- Republic of Vietnam Gallantry Cross Unit Citation	Level of award (cited before the Regiment) and additional awards
74	Star, 3/8", Gold	ARMY- Republic of Vietnam Gallantry Cross Unit Citation	Level of award (cited before the Corps) and additional awards
75	Star, 3/8", Silver	ARMY- Republic of Vietnam Gallantry Cross Unit Citation	Level of award (cited before the Division) and additional awards
76	Target, Pistol, Gold	COAST GUARD- Pistol Marksmanship Ribbon	Recipient of Distinguished Pistol Shot Badge
77	Target, Pistol, Gold	COAST GUARD- Pistol Marksmanship Ribbon	Recipient of Distinguished Marksman Badge

11. MEDAL CLASPS & BARS

The appearance of medal bars and clasps to reward subsequent acts of heroism/meritorious service or to commemorate participation in specific battles or campaigns seems to have coincided, once again, with the ascendence of the British Empire in the early 19th century.

As previously described, the "additional award" bar was instituted in 1856 along with the creation of the Victoria Cross. However the battle clasp, which rewards participation in single military campaigns, had its beginnings much earlier when Great Britain instituted the Army Gold Cross in 1810. The Royal Warrant of the time established a series of ornate gold clasps, containing the name of the specific engagement, which were attached to the suspension ribbon.

The practice made its U.S. debut in 1898 with the appearance of engagement bars to the Sampson Medal and was followed shortly thereafter by the extensive series of battle and service clasps issued with the World War I Victory Medal (see inset for typical examples). No device was authorized for wear on the ribbon bar of the Sampson Medal to denote receipt of these clasps but "battle stars" were extensively used on the ribbon bar of the Victory Medal, one for each battle clasp received.

| Sampson Medal | World War I Victory Medal |

Plate 17 depicts the bars and clasps that are most applicable to the intended time frame of this book:

(1) The individual Services issued a series of clasps to the American Defense Service Medal which indicated that the wearer was serving outside the Continental U.S. prior to America's entry into World War II. A 3/16" diameter bronze star was worn on the ribbon bar to indicate the receipt of any of these clasps (see also the reference to the bronze letter "A" under the "Attachments and Devices" section of this book).

(2) The Army of Occupation Medal, issued at the end of World War II, is always worn with one or both of the depicted

bars to indicate the area in which the recipient served. It is to be noted that no ribbon device was issued to denote the receipt of either or both clasps.

(3) As can be seen, The Navy Occupation Medal was issued with two differently-named clasps but all of the above comments on the Army medal apply equally to the Navy version.

(4) In the only case of a battle clasp being named for a specific World War II engagement, the Navy and Marine Corps issued a bar to those military personnel who participated in the heroic defense of Wake Island from 7th to 22nd December, 1941. The clasp is worn on the suspension ribbon of the appropriate Expeditionary Medal and is represented by a silver letter "W" on the ribbon bar.

(5) Military personnel who volunteer to spend a winter on the Antarctic continent may wear a bronze clasp entitled: "Wintered Over" on the suspension ribbon of the Antarctica Service Medal. For a second such period of service, a gold bar containing the same inscription is awarded and for any hearty soul willing to endure a third winter, a similar clasp in silver is bestowed. Only the most senior bar is worn on the suspension ribbon. The bars are represented on the ribbon bar by a disk depicting the Antarctic continent in the same finish as the clasp.

(6) Although not strictly of a military nature, the most ornate clasp in the U.S. repertoire is the second award bar to the Department of Transportation's Life Saving Medals. As before, the finish of the bar corresponds to the actual medal, gold or silver, which was awarded. When the width of all U.S. ribbons was standardized in the 1950's, both Life Saving Medals were redesigned. At the same time, the clasp was scaled down to conform with the new 1 3/8" ribbon width and also underwent a minor date change.

(7) The Army Good Conduct Medal uses a unique series of bars in three finishes (bronze, silver and gold) to denote additional awards. Borrowing from the slang expression for a reenlistment ("signing on for another hitch") the clasp, worn on <u>both</u> the suspension ribbon and the ribbon bar, features rope ("half-hitch") knots to indicate the number of times the recipient has reenlisted.

(8) And finally, there is the "Little Bar That Never Was", a classic case of an over-eager bureaucrat jumping the proverbial gun. This bar, inscribed "Fleet Marine", was discovered on an official U.S. Government wall chart of awards and decorations dated 1967 and was intended for wear by Naval personnel who served with Marine Corps units in combat. It was evidently superseded by the present miniature Marine Corps emblem without fanfare, leaving the chart makers with entire omelettes on their faces.

Plate 17 - Medal Clasps of World War II and Beyond

★ FOREIGN SERVICE ★

Army

SEA

Coast Guard

FLEET

Navy

BASE

Navy

(1) American Defense Service Medal

JAPAN

GERMANY

(2) Army of Occupation Medal

EUROPE

ASIA

(3) Navy Occupation Service Medal

WAKE ISLAND

(4) Navy/Marine Corps
Expeditionary Medals

WINTERED OVER

(5) Antarctica
Service Medal

SECOND SERVICE
ACT OF CONGRESS MAY 4th 1882

Prior to 1949

SECOND SERVICE
ACT OF CONGRESS AUG 4th 1949

1949 and Thereafter

(6) Gold and Silver Life Saving Medals

(7) Army Good Conduct
Medal

FLEET MARINE

(8) The "Little Bar that
Never Was"

Note: All illustrations are shown oversized for clarity

12. UNDERSTANDING U.S. AWARDS

The evolution of the awards system of the United States may be best characterized as paralleling the American passion for individual freedom. To the casual observer, it might resemble an endless series of unrelated regulations designed to confuse rather than to inform, but upon closer examination, one finds a highly-organized, well-documented system that has been overcomplicated by historical inertia.

When this country won its independence from Great Britain, most British traditions were retained but all trappings of the old regal system were repudiated. As a result, almost 75 years elapsed between the adoption of the U.S. Constitution and the authorization of our first military award, the Medal of Honor. At that time, however, Congress made no provision for a centralized authority to govern awards that may be established in the future. Whether this was due to persistent fears of an "Imperial Presidency" or purely through oversight is still unclear, but once the War and Navy Departments initiated their own systems of decorations and campaign/service medals, it was evident that our Head of State was not even nominally responsible for the execution of the U.S. awards policy (The President traditionally presents the Medal of Honor but does so in the name of the Congress).

As the number of awards grew, responsibility for the approval and presentation of an award to a recipient became (and remains today) a function of the importance of the proposed award. As in most Armed Services around the world, the immediate field commander is empowered to nominate deserving candidates for an appropriate medal but here the resemblance ends. In the U.S. Army, for example, final award authority can be a Company, Regimental, Brigade or Division Commander providing the award is for a campaign, good conduct, achievement, commendation or meritorious service. Only when the upper strata of the "Pyramid of Honor" are attained (i.e., Bronze Star Medal and above) is the senior level of command (The Chief of Staff, Secretary of the Army or Secretary of Defense) required to act upon such recommendations. The other Services follow this pattern closely, some going even further by delegating the authority to issue a few of the more senior awards to lower echelon commanders during wartime situations.

Having thus created their own historical precedent, the individual Services went on to establish distinct and unique regulations for the display of decorations, medals and service ribbons, a policy that lasted from its Civil War beginnings through the World War II era.

In 1947, when the U.S. Armed Forces were unified into the present Department of Defense, one might have expected a series of orderly and clear-cut directives that would totally reorganize all such awards policies. However, with only a few notable exceptions, (e.g., standardization of the height and width of ribbons plus some award criteria) this has not been the case.

Although Joint Service awards committees do exist, they can only recommend general policies for those items shared by all the Armed Forces, but do NOT have the authority to set standards within the individual Services. As a result, some 78 new awards have been authorized since unification, only 19 of which are common to all the Services and the rules governing the display of ribbons and devices now vary so widely as to require a road map.

1. Order of Precedence

The first area of potential confusion is the order of ribbon wear on the U.S. military uniform. A careful examination of the various awards manuals and uniform regulations shows that three distinct arrangements exist among the five Services (the Navy, Marine Corps and Coast Guard share a common scheme).

Arbitrarily taking the Navy method as a baseline, the various award precedence schemes break down into general categories as follows:

A. U.S. Military Decorations
B. U.S. Unit Awards
C. U.S. Non-Military Decorations (e.g.: Presidential Medal of Freedom, awards of NASA, NOAA, USPHS, etc.)
D. U.S. Merchant Marine Decorations
E. Prisoner of War and Good Conduct Medals
F. Campaign, Service and Training Awards
G. U.S. Merchant Marine Service Awards
H. Foreign Military Decorations
I. Foreign Unit Awards
J. Non-U.S. Service Awards
K. Marksmanship Awards

The precedence established by the Army is as follows:

A. U.S. Military Decorations
E. Prisoner of War Medal
C. U.S. Non-Military Decorations
E. Good Conduct Medal
F. Campaign, Service and Training Awards
D. U.S. Merchant Marine Decorations
G. U.S. Merchant Marine Service Awards
H. Foreign Military Decorations
J. Non-U.S. Service Awards

NOTE: All U.S. and foreign unit awards (categories B and I above) are worn on the right breast of the Army uniform.

The Air Force has been left for last owing to its unique set of ribbon rules. Not only is the Air Force arrangement different from those discussed earlier but some of their medals and ribbons, designated as "Achievement Awards", do not fit neatly into the previously-defined categories. The Air Force precedence list is as follows:

A. U.S. Military Decorations
B. U.S. Unit Awards
C. U.S. Non-Military Decorations
D. U.S. Merchant Marine Decorations
E. Prisoner of War Medal
-- Combat Readiness Medal
E. Good Conduct Medal
F. Campaign, Service and Training Awards
K. Marksmanship Awards
-- Air Force Training Ribbon
J. Philippine Service Awards
G. U.S. Merchant Marine Service Awards
H. Foreign Military Decorations
I. Foreign Unit Awards
J. Non-U.S. Service Awards

2. Campaign, Service & Training Awards

In the area of campaign, service and training awards, the Services have again developed different rules and regulations. Air Force award regulations, for example, are roughly chronological, progressing to the present time as follows:

1. Air Reserve Forces Meritorious Service Medal
2. Outstanding Airman of the Year Ribbon
3. Air Force Recognition Ribbon
4. China Service Medal
5. American Defense Service Medal
6. Women's Army Corps Service Medal
7. World War II Campaign Medals (worn in order earned)
8. World War II Victory Medal
9. World War II Occupation Medal
10. Medal for Humane Action
11. National Defense Service Medal
12. Korean Service Medal
13. Antarctica Service Medal
14. Armed Forces Expeditionary Medal
15. Vietnam Service Medal
16. Southwest Asia Service Medal
17. Armed Forces Service Medal
18. Humanitarian Service Medal
19. Outstanding Volunteer Service Medal
20. Overseas Ribbon (Short Tour)
21. Overseas Ribbon (Long Tour)
22. Longevity Service Award Ribbon
23. Armed Forces Reserve Medal
24. NCO Professional Military Education Graduate Ribbon
25. Basic Military Education Honor Graduate Ribbon

According to applicable Army directives, campaign, service and training awards are worn as follows:

1. Reserve Components Achievement Medal
2. American Defense Service Medal
3. Women's Army Corps Service Medal
4. American Campaign Medal
5. Asiatic-Pacific Campaign Medal
6. European-African-Middle Eastern Campaign Medal
7. World War II Victory Medal

8. Army of Occupation Medal (World War II)
9. Medal for Humane Action
10. National Defense Service Medal
11. Korean Service Medal
12. Antarctica Service Medal
13. Armed Forces Expeditionary Medal
14. Vietnam Service Medal
15. Southwest Asia Service Medal
16. Armed Forces Service Medal
17. Humanitarian Service Medal
18. Outstanding Volunteer Service Medal
19. Armed Forces Reserve Medal
20. NCO Professional Development Ribbon
21. Army Service Ribbon
22. Overseas Service Ribbon
23. Reserve Components Overseas Training Ribbon

Similarly, the Navy, Marine Corps and Coast Guard have assigned each ribbon a specific slot regardless of the dates of service as follows:

1. Naval Reserve Meritorious Service Medal
2. Selected Marine Corps Reserve Medal
3. Coast Guard Reserve Good Conduct Medal
4. Fleet Marine Force Ribbon (Navy only)
5. Navy/Marine Corps Expeditionary Medals
6. China Service Medal
7. American Defense Service Medal
8. American Campaign Medal
9. European-African-Middle Eastern Campaign Medal
10. Asiatic-Pacific Campaign Medal
11. World War II Victory Medal
12. U.S. Antarctic Expedition Medal
13. Navy Occupation Service Medal (World War II)
14. Medal for Humane Action
15. National Defense Service Medal
16. Korean Service Medal
17. Antarctica Service Medal
18. Arctic Service Medal (Coast Guard only)
19. Armed Forces Expeditionary Medal
20. Vietnam Service Medal
21. Southwest Asia Service Medal
22. Armed Forces Service Medal
23. Humanitarian Service Medal
24. Outstanding Volunteer Service Medal
25. Sea Service Deployment Ribbon (Navy, Marine Corps only)
26. Arctic Service Ribbon (Navy, Marine Corps only)
27. Naval Reserve Sea Service Ribbon
28. Overseas Service Ribbon (Navy, Marine Corps only)
29. Recruiting Service Ribbon (Navy Only)
30. Recruiting Ribbon (Marine Corps Only)
31. Special Operations Service Ribbon (Coast Guard only)
32. Sea Service Ribbon (Coast Guard only)
33. Restricted Duty Ribbon (Coast Guard only)
34. Basic Training Honor Graduate Ribbon (Coast Guard only)
35. Armed Forces Reserve Medal
36. Naval Reserve Medal
37. Marine Corps Reserve Ribbon

Although this makes a foolproof method for checking a ribbon display during a full-dress inspection, it has also created the following anomalies:

A. The China Service Medal (Extended) is worn before all World War II service awards in spite of the prescribed dates of service (1945-57).

B. The U.S. Antarctic Expedition Medal is worn after all World War II ribbons although the qualifying dates lie between 1939 and 1941.

C. World War II Area/Campaign Medals are worn in the specific order shown regardless of when earned. This is also true for the Army which seems to favor alphabetical order for the three awards.

D. The Antarctica Service and Coast Guard Arctic Service Medals are worn after the Korean Service Medal although the service may have been performed as early as 1946.

E. The Navy and Marine Corps Expeditionary Medals take precedence over all except the oldest campaign awards with no regard for dates of service, the most recent being rescue/evacuation efforts in Haiti.

3. Display of Attachments/Devices

The Services have gone their separate ways in the prescribed arrangement of the various devices used on the ribbons of decorations and service awards. Section 10 (pages 51-57) describes all devices used on U.S. ribbons, but of particular interest are the following:

A. Additional award and campaign devices
B. Bronze Letter "V"
C. Differences in device usage
D. Multiplicity of device types (ribbon clutter)

A. Additional Award and Campaign Devices

In case A, bronze/gold stars and oak leaf clusters have been used to denote campaign participation and additional awards since World War I (see plates 22 and 23 for proper usage of these devices). However, the regulations have created a disparity in the use of the silver device worn in lieu of five bronze devices. For example, The Army and Air Force direct that a silver oak leaf cluster be worn to the right (i.e., the wearer's right) of all bronze clusters on the same ribbon.

The Navy and Coast Guard, on the other hand, have dictated that "a silver star shall be located as near the center of the ribbon as a symmetrical arrangement will permit". They also specify that any bronze or gold star on the same ribbon be "placed to the wearer's right" of the silver star. The Marine Corps has chosen to reverse this procedure and requires the bronze or gold star to be placed on the wearer's LEFT of any silver star.

Because of these conflicting directives, the ribbon

configurations depicted in Plate 18 are required. As can be seen, Navy and Marine Corps devices group around the silver star, while the Army and Air Force move the silver oak leaf cluster to the wearer's right as a new bronze cluster is added.

In almost identical fashion, the grouping of devices ("battle stars") on campaign awards is governed by the various regulations to produce the configurations shown in Plate 19.

B. Bronze Letter "V"

With reference to case B, the bronze letter "V" (Combat Distinguishing Device) not only has various methods of wear, but the Services vary widely on the ribbons to which it may be attached. It is prescribed in common for use on the Bronze Star and Joint Service Commendation Medals but beyond that point, the usage variations in Table I are seen:

Plate 20 shows how the device is worn on the ribbon bar according to the applicable regulations. At first glance, the schemes might appear identical to that used for decorations (Plate 18). However, there is now a subtle difference since the Navy, Marine Corps and Coast Guard require that letter devices be absolutely centered on the ribbon bar. The Army and Air Force, as before, move the letter further to the wearer's right as each new oak leaf cluster is added. In the case of the Air Medal, as awarded by the Army, the letter and the prescribed numerals are arranged symmetrically on the ribbon bar.

However, even the "absolutely centered" rule has a variation. If either the Coast Guard Commendation Medal or Achievement Medal is authorized with BOTH the letters "V" and "O" (Operational Distinguishing Device), the two devices are worn on either side of the central white stripe.

Finally, there is the case where all the previously-discussed conditions come together and the letter "V" is displayed with the silver and gold or bronze additional award devices (see Plate 21). As before, the letter is the senior device in the Army and Air Force displays but, in another quick turnabout, all the Naval-related Services are now in total agreement.

C. Differences in Device Usage

As for case C, the following are examples of conflicting directives in the use of devices:

1. Originally, an additional award of the National Defense Service Medal was denoted by an oak leaf cluster on the Army version and a small (3/16") bronze star by all the other Services. The bronze star is now used universally.

2. The Army and Air Force use the bronze arrowhead device on the ribbons of the World War II and Korean campaigns and, in the case of the Army, the Vietnam War and Armed Forces Expeditionary Medal (for the Grenada and Panama Operations). Although active participation in assault landings is part of the Navy's mission, they have never authorized the wear of this device.

Plate 18- Placement of Silver Devices on the Ribbon Bar

NO. OF AWARDS	NAVY and COAST GUARD	MARINE CORPS	ARMY	AIR FORCE
6	☆	☆	🍃	🍃
7	★ ☆	☆ ★	🍃 🍃	🍃 🍃
8	★ ★ ★	★ ★ ★	🍃 🍃 🍃	🍃 🍃 🍃
9	★ ★ ★ ★	★ ★ ★ ★	🍃 🍃 🍃 🍃	🍃 🍃 🍃 🍃
10	★ ★ ★ ★ ★	★ ★ ★ ★ ★	SEE NOTE 1	SEE NOTE 2

Legend: ★ = 3/16" Bronze or 5/16" Gold Star

☆ = 3/16" or 5/16" Silver Star

🍃 = Bronze Oak Leaf Cluster

🍃 = Silver Oak Leaf Cluster

NOTES: 1. Army regulations limit the number of oak leaf clusters which may be worn on a single ribbon to a maximum of four (4).

2. Air Force regulations limit the number of devices which may be worn on a single ribbon to a maximum of four (4). If more than four devices are authorized, a second ribbon is worn containing the excess devices.

Plate 19- Placement of Silver Campaign Stars on the Ribbon Bar

NO. OF CAMPAIGNS	NAVY and COAST GUARD	MARINE CORPS	ARMY	AIR FORCE
5	☆	☆	☆	☆
6	★ ☆	☆ ★	☆ ★	☆ ★
7	★ ☆ ★	★ ☆ ★	☆ ★ ★	☆ ★ ★
8	★ ★ ☆ ★	★ ☆ ★ ★	☆ ★ ★ ★	☆ ★ ★ ★
9	★ ★ ☆ ★ ★	★ ★ ☆ ★ ★	☆ ★ ★ ★ ★	SEE NOTE

Legend: ★ = 3/16" Bronze Star
         ☆ = 3/16" Silver Star

NOTES: 1. Air Force regulations limit the number of devices which may be worn on a single ribbon to a maximum of four (4). If more than four devices are authorized, a second ribbon is worn containing the excess devices.

2. Campaign stars are often referred to as "Battle Stars".

Plate 20- Placement of the Bronze Letter "V" on the Ribbon Bar

	NAVY, MARINE CORPS AND COAST GUARD	ARMY	AIR FORCE
NO. OF AWARDS			
1	**V**	**V**	**V**
2	★ **V**	**V** 🍂	**V** 🍂
3	★ **V** ★	**V** 🍂🍂	**V** 🍂🍂
4	★★**V**★	**V** 🍂🍂🍂	**V** 🍂🍂🍂
5	★★**V**★★	**V**🍂🍂🍂🍂	SEE NOTE

Legend: **V** = Bronze Letter "V"

★ = 5/16" dia. Gold Star

🍂 = Bronze Oak Leaf Cluster

NOTE: Air Force regulations limit the number of devices which may be worn on a single ribbon to a maximum of four (4). If more than four devices are authorized, a second ribbon is worn containing the excess devices.

Plate 21- Placement of the Letter "V" With Other Ribbon Devices

NO. OF AWARDS	NAVY, MARINE CORPS AND COAST GUARD	ARMY	AIR FORCE
6	★ **V**	**V** 🍂	**V** 🍂
7	★ **V** ★	**V** 🍂 🍂	**V** 🍂 🍂
8	★★**V**★	**V** 🍂 🍂 🍂	**V** 🍂 🍂 🍂
9	★★**V**★★	**V** 🍂 🍂 🍂 🍂	SEE NOTE 2
10	★★★**V**★★	SEE NOTE 1	SEE NOTE 2

Legend: **V**   = Bronze Letter "V"
☆   = 5/16" dia. Silver Star
★   = 5/16" dia. Gold Star
🍂   = Silver Oak Leaf Cluster
🍂   = Bronze Oak Leaf Cluster

NOTES: 1.   Army regulations limit the number of oak leaf clusters which may be worn on a single ribbon to a maximum of four (4).

2.   Air Force regulations limit the number of devices which may be worn on a single ribbon to a maximum of four (4). If more than four devices are authorized, a second ribbon is worn containing the excess devices.

Table I - Usage Variations of the Bronze Letter "V"

SERVICE(S)	APPLICABLE MEDALS
Army	Air Medal, Commendation Medal
Navy, Marine Corps	Legion of Merit, Distinguished Flying Cross, Air Medal, Commendation Medal, Achievement Medal (<u>Note</u>: The "V" was no longer awarded with the Legion of Merit and Achievement Medal after the Vietnam War but was reinstituted for awards of the two medals during Operation Desert Storm and thereafter)
Coast Guard	Legion of Merit, Commendation Medal, Achievement Medal
Air Force	Outstanding Unit Award, Organizational Excellence Award

3. The Navy uses the small (3/16") bronze star on its unit awards (i.e., Unit Commendation, Meritorious Unit Commendation and "E" Ribbon) as an additional award device. The Coast Guard, however, uses the <u>large</u> (5/16") gold star on its equivalent unit awards.

4. Until the Department of Defense standardized the practice, most of the Services used a system of bronze numerals to indicate additional awards of the Humanitarian Service Medal. From the outset, however, the Coast Guard utilized small (3/16") bronze and silver stars to denote one and five additional awards of the medal respectively. It is the Coast Guard system that is now in effect for <u>all</u> Branches of the Service (Plate 22).

5. Contrary to other policies covering personal and unit awards, no provisions are made to denote the fifth and subsequent awards of the Navy "E" Ribbon. Upon receipt of the fourth award, the wreathed, silver "E" is worn and <u>no further devices</u> may be affixed to the ribbon after that.

6. Unlike any other Service, the Coast Guard forbids the wear of the oak leaf cluster on its uniform. This requires the substitution of a large (5/16") gold or silver star to denote additional awards of any Joint Service decoration (e.g., DDSM, DSSM, DMSM, JSCM, JSAM) or any award(s) earned while part of the Army or Air Force.

7. The Army permits the wear of devices on the Republic of Vietnam Gallantry Cross Unit Citation (bronze palms plus gold, silver and/or bronze stars) to denote the level of the award as well as subsequent awards. The other Services only allow the display of a single bronze palm.

D. Multiplicity of Device Types

Case D arises from the fact that many different devices can be worn on the same ribbon. Although two might be acceptable, (e.g., letter "V" with gold star, arrowhead with battle star, etc.), things are definitely out of hand when as many as THREE distinct device types can be affixed to the

same ribbon. The most extreme examples in the ribbon clutter category are the following:

1. The Navy, which permits the wear of the Presidential Unit Citation with a gold letter "N", a gold globe and a bronze star at the same time.

2. The Coast Guard, which authorizes the simultaneous display of a bronze letter "V", 5/16" gold/silver stars and a silver letter "O" on the ribbons of its Commendation and Achievement Medals.

3. The Marine Corps, which uses a 3/16" bronze star or 5/16" gold and silver stars plus bronze numerals, gold numerals and the bronze letter "V" simultaneously on the Air Medal (see the next section for a more complete discussion of Air Medal device utilization).

4. Air Medal Devices

Still on the general subject of ribbon appurtenances, we shall now turn our attention to the case of the Air Medal, the classic example of how many different ways the Services can specify the wearing of devices, both now and in the past. As mentioned in the previous section, both the Army and the Navy use the bronze letter "V" on the Air Medal but it is in denoting additional awards that the Services have demonstrated some real Yankee individuality.

Although the Army and Air Force systems (i.e., numerals and oak leaf clusters, respectively) are totally different, they are, at the very least, straightforward and easily understood. It is the Navy, then, that has entered a new dimension by establishing two very distinct categories, strike/ flight and individual service, for all awards of the Air Medal, both initial and subsequent.

Strike/flight awards of the Navy Air Medal are indicated by bronze block numerals worn on the right-hand orange stripe (as seen by the viewer). For individual awards, a small (3/16" dia.) bronze star is used to indicate the first award while the traditional 5/16" gold stars are used to denote additional individual awards (see Plate 23).

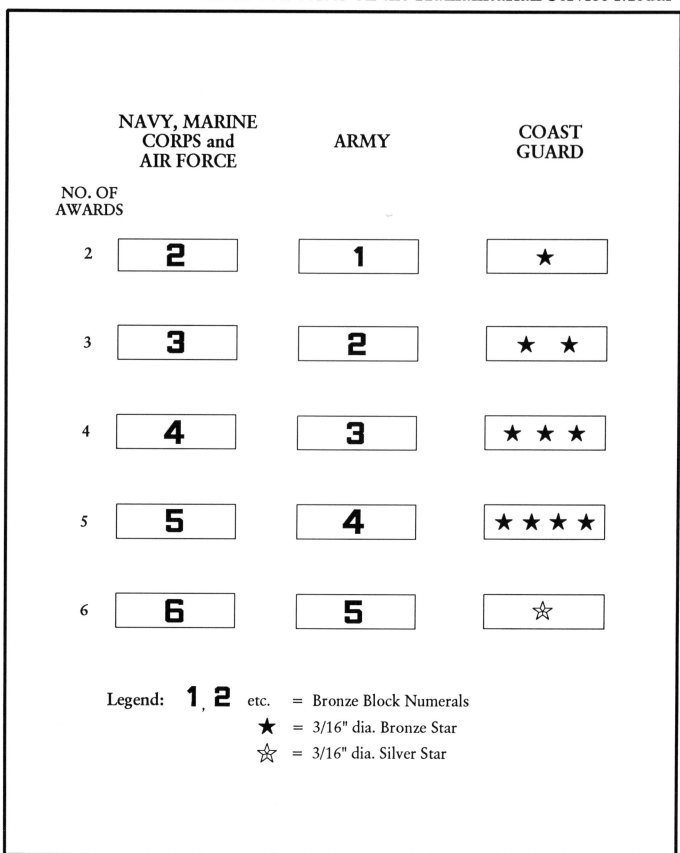

Plate 23- Placement of Devices on the Air Medal Ribbon

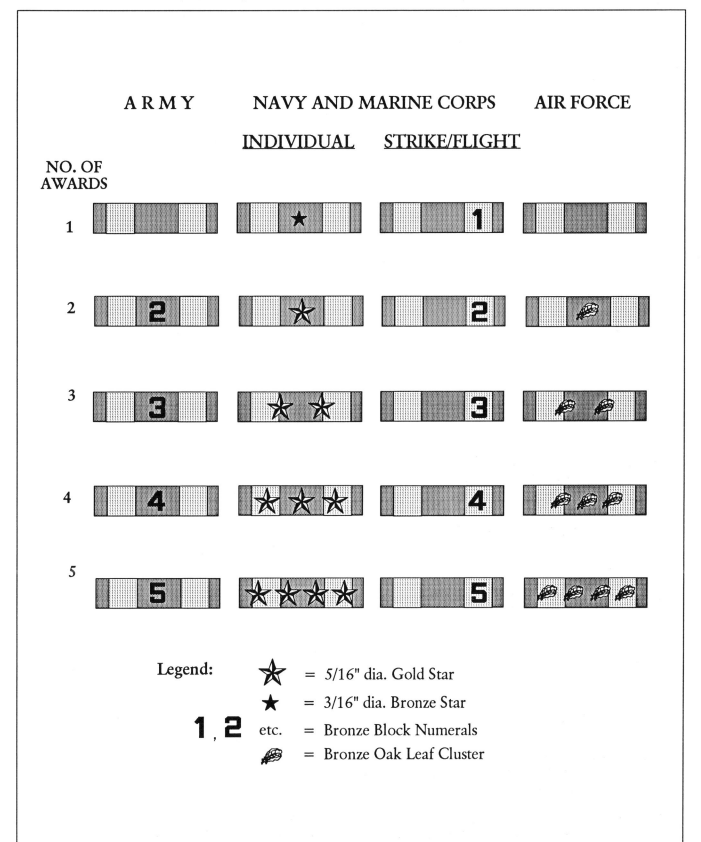

The two different categories have created a situation in which a device is used on a ribbon to denote INITIAL award of a personal decoration, the first in American medallic history (for purists, it will be noted that the Merchant Marine Gallant Ship Citation Bar is issued with a silver seahorse device and the Navy "E" Ribbon carries a silver letter "E" upon initial issue. Both of these, however, are <u>unit awards</u> rather than decorations).

Just for the record, the Navy had used the above method for many years but discarded it in favor of a system that utilized gold block numerals, placed on the left-hand orange stripe (as seen by the viewer) to denote the total number of individual awards of the Air Medal (see Plate 24).

Both of the above cases were combined with the bronze strike/flight numerals as described above. Use of the gold numerals was not universal, however, and was resisted vigorously by those senior officers who clung tenaciously to their gold stars. So, with the demise of the gold numeral, there is now another body of dissatisfied Navy men. These are the Vietnam-era pilots who earned the medal in great profusion, but now have great difficulty in displaying their true number of awards using 5/16" gold and silver stars.

The Coast Guard uses ONLY the 5/16" gold and silver stars to denote additional awards of the Air Medal for all categories of heroic and meritorious achievement in flight. However, strike/flight awards received while serving with Navy units may be worn on the ribbon as prescribed above.

And to close the subject on a final note of confusion, the Marine Corps follows the Navy's lead in using numerals and bronze, gold and silver stars but also allows any gold numerals earned prior to 1989 to be worn on the ribbon.

5. Disparate Regulations

As the next chapter in this "Dissertation on Diversity", the following differences in ribbon wear between the various Armed Services are submitted without further comment:

A. The Air Force is the only Branch of the Service to authorize the wear of miniature ribbon bars on the uniform, albeit restricted to the lightweight summer shirt.

B. The Air Force permits a second ribbon to be worn if more than four (4) devices are authorized for wear on a single ribbon bar. The Army also specifies a limit of four (4) oak leaf clusters on the ribbon bar but this leaves the question of a 10th award up in the air since the hypothetical recipient has no way to display the requisite one silver and four bronze oak leaf clusters.

C. Unit awards worn by Army personnel are unique in that the gold frames are physically larger (1/2" vs. 3/8" high) and are worn on the right breast of the Army uniform. This regulation is also applicable to unit awards received from other Services or from foreign governments. If this seems unusual, consider the original Army scheme (circa 1960)

that placed the Presidential Unit Citation on the right breast, other U.S. unit awards on the left breast amongst the other ribbons, foreign unit citations <u>below</u> all other ribbons on the left breast pocket <u>flap</u> and the Meritorious Unit Commendation in the form of a sew-on patch on the lower right-hand sleeve.

D. The Navy, Marine Corps and Coast Guard follow the "right-side" precedent to a limited extent, requiring ribbons that have no associated medals (e.g., Combat Action, Unit, Marksmanship, etc.) to be worn on the right breast on those occasions when full-sized medals are authorized. But, as before, there is disagreement on the order of wear. The Marine Corps requires a "top to bottom, wearer's right to wearer's left" arrangement while the Navy and Coast Guard specify an "inboard to outboard" display (see Section 8). By contrast, neither the Army nor the Air Force permits these "ribbon-only" awards to be worn on the uniform when full-size or miniature medals are specified.

E. The Army and the Coast Guard Uniform Regulations stipulate that unit awards with gold frames be worn with the laurel leaves on the frame pointing up. The Marine Corps accomplishes the same goal by requiring the laurel leaves to form a "V" (point down). On the other hand, none of the other awards or uniform regulations mention the subject.

F. The Army is the only Service to permit the wear of unit awards by personnel who did not participate in the action for which it was cited. Any individual joining at a later date may wear the unit award while permanently attached, but must relinquish it upon subsequent reassignment.

G. Army and Marine Corps ribbons may, at the wearer's option, be worn with a 1/8" separation between adjacent rows. The other Services do not permit any such separation.

H. Similarly, the maximum number of ribbons that may be displayed in each row depends on which Service is being discussed. The applicable quotes from the various uniform regulations are offered in Table II without comment:

I. The Marine Corps, in an unfortunate reference to the senior status of the color blue in heraldry, specifies the wear of the ribbon for the Merchant Marine Mariner's Medal in the order of blue, white, red (as seen by an observer) thus putting themselves out of step with all of the other Services as well as the dictates of the awarding agency itself.

J. On a number of occasions, the Services have awarded more than one medal for the <u>same</u> combat action as per Table III.

K. Then consider the refusal of some Services to permit the wear of certain awards of the other Branches. As of this writing, the restrictions existing are shown in Table IV.

L. The Coast Guard, being the hereditary "owners" of the Department of Transportation (originally the Treasury

Plate 24- Former Device Usage on the Navy Air Medal

NAVY AND MARINE CORPS
(INDIVIDUAL AWARDS)

	(CIRCA 1966-1978)	(CIRCA 1978-1991)
NO. OF AWARDS		
1		
2		
3		
4		
5		

Legend:

⭐ = 5/16" dia. Gold Star

★ = 3/16" dia. Bronze Star

1 , 2 etc. = Gold Block Numerals

Table II - Regulations for Ribbon Wear

SERVICE	REGULATIONS FOR RIBBON WEAR
ARMY:	• No line will contain more than four service ribbons • Unit awards will be worn with not more than three per row
NAVY:	• Worn in horizontal rows of three each
MARINE CORPS:	• Normally worn in rows of three, but rows of four may be worn when displaying a large number of awards
COAST GUARD:	• One, two or three ribbons are worn in a single row
AIR FORCE:	• Wear ribbons in multiples of three or four

Department) Gold and Silver Lifesaving Medals, treats these awards as military decorations. As can be seen in the Coast Guard ribbon chest (Plate 13) they are afforded a specific position in the Coast Guard order of precedence. All other Services, however, consider them to be non-military decorations with no absolute precedence within the group.

M. As another sidelight to this discussion, the Coast Guard is alone in specifying an additional award device (the large 5/16" gold star) for the Lifesaving Medals.

N. Coast Guard is also the only Service to include awards to civilians in its list of military decorations. The cases in point are the three Department of Transportation awards listed in Plate 13 which may be worn as shown on the uniform.

O. Finally, the ultimate in awards with little significance is the Army Service Ribbon. Since this ribbon is awarded to all officers or enlisted men who have successfully completed any entry-level training course, EVERY PERSON in the U.S. Army is entitled to wear it. Unlike a true general service award (e.g., National Defense Service Medal), the Army Service Ribbon has no termination date and requires no "service" of any kind.

6. Strange Common Regulations

Thus far, this section has dealt only with the differences between the various U.S. awards regulations. As a final chapter, it would have been refreshing to report that the remaining areas, in which the Services all agree amongst themselves, made absolute sense from the standpoints of logic and tradition. Unfortunately, this is not the case as can be seen in the following examples:

A. The medals associated with the Philippine Defense, Liberation and Independence Ribbons, although issued and sanctioned for wear by a friendly foreign government, may not be worn on the U.S. military uniform. All of the applicable Uniform Regulations refer to these awards as "Ribbons" rather than "Medals" and permit only the ribbon to be worn.

B. Ribbon devices, in most cases, are worn to denote the award of clasps to certain service medals (e.g., World War I Victory Medal, American Defense Service Medal, Navy Expeditionary Medal, etc.). The sole exception to the rule is the World War II Occupation Medal, which makes no provisions for a device in cases where both clasps have been awarded.

C. The distinctive ribbons associated with certain United Nations medals may not be worn on the U.S. military uniform. Military personnel who took part in the Western New Guinea (UNTEA) or India/Pakistan (UNMOGIP) operations as well as the latest excursions into Somalia, Haiti and Bosnia must wear the "standard" U.N. Observer ribbon normally associated with the UNTSO and UNOGIL medals (light blue with a single white stripe near each edge). This policy is under study by the Department of Defense as of this writing.

D. A second award of the Philippine Presidential Unit Citation (for service during disaster relief operations in 1972) is denoted by a small bronze star on the ribbon. However, a similar second award of the Republic of Korea Presidential Unit Citation for the same operation goes unrecognized.

E. Finally, consider the case of the "Wintered Over" clasps and disks used on the Antarctica Service Medal. In a classic example of reverse logic, the time-honored sequence of bronze, silver and gold was altered to bronze-gold-silver to denote 1, 2, and 3 winters respectively.

Table III - Occasions on Which Multiple Awards Were Authorized

DATE	EVENT/ACTION	AWARDS PRESENTED
1937	Attack on Gunboat "Panay" (China)	1. Navy Expeditionary Medal 2. China Service Medal
1941	Defense of Wake Island	1. Asiatic-Pacific Campaign Medal 2. Navy (or Marine Corps) Expeditionary Medal with "Wake Island" clasp 3. Navy Presidential Unit Citation
1941	Defense of the Philippine Islands (U.S. Army personnel)	1. Bronze Star Medal 2. Asiatic-Pacific Campaign Medal 3. Army Presidential Unit Citation 4. Philippine Defense Ribbon (Philippine Government)
1975	Evacuation of Saigon, Republic of Vietnam	1. Armed Forces Expeditionary Medal 2. Humanitarian Service Medal 3. (Some personnel): Combat Action Ribbon plus Navy Unit Commendation or Navy Meritorious Unit Commendation

Table IV - Inter-Service Restrictions on Ribbon Wear

SERVICE	RESTRICTIONS
ARMY	(a) Air Force Longevity Service Award Ribbon (b) Air Force and Navy Marksmanship ribbons (c) Marksmanship Badges awarded by other U.S. Services
MARINE CORPS	(a) Army Combat Medical or Combat Infantryman's Badge must be "traded in" for the Combat Action Ribbon (b) Any award that has no direct Marine Corps equivalent (e.g., Navy Marksmanship Ribbons, Air Force Training and Recognition Ribbons, Army Service Ribbon, etc.)
NAVY	(a) Army badges per the Marine Corps (above) (b) Coast Guard Commandant's Letter of Commendation Ribbon (c) All other awards having no direct Navy equivalent.
COAST GUARD	(a) All training and marksmanship medals/badges/ribbons earned in another branch of the Service. (b) Any award that has no direct Coast Guard equivalent (e.g., Air Force Longevity Service Award Ribbon, Combat Readiness Medal, etc.)
AIR FORCE	(a) No comparable restrictions instituted.

13. NOTES AND COMMENTS

As indicated in the Introduction to this book, certain errors/omissions have been noted by the authors subsequent to the preparation of the color plates. In addition, there are certain areas of text which require further clarification where space was at a premium. These will be referenced to the applicable page(s).

Page 19: The Coast Guard's latest (and most senior) award is the Transportation Distinguished Service Medal (see ribbon on page 46) which was approved too late for inclusion in this book. It takes precedence over the Coast Guard Distinguished Service Medal and is awarded "...by the Secretary of Transportation to a member of the Coast Guard who has provided exceptionally meritorious service in a duty of great responsibility while assigned to the Department of Transportation...". It has already been named the "Commandant's Medal" since its award is expected to be limited to the most senior echelons of the Coast Guard. With a projection of only one award per year, it may already rank with some of the rarest awards in the world.

Transportation Distinguished
Service Medal

Page 21, Items 20 and 26: Lifesaving medals are awarded to military personnel only if the individual is on a leave or liberty status. Otherwise, a military decoration is more appropriate.

Page 21, Item 21: The Bronze Star Medal for meritorious service was authorized for those awarded either the Combat Infantryman Badge or Combat Medical Badge between 7 December 1941 and 2 September 1945. Since the two badges were not awarded until July, 1943, those Army infantrymen and medics whose meritorious achievements in combat prior to July, 1943 are confirmable in writing may still be eligible for the Bronze Star.

Page 23, Item 29: The Army Commendation Medal, originally a ribbon only, is authorized for award to any Army member who received a letter or certificate of commendation signed by a Major General or higher for meritorious achievement between 7 December 1941 and 1 January 1946.

Page 23, Item 30: The Navy Commendation Medal is authorized for award to any member of the U.S. Navy, Marine Corps or Coast Guard who has received a letter of commendation from the Secretary of the Navy, the Commander in Chief of the Pacific or Atlantic Fleet or Commander of the Fleet Marine Force, Pacific for an act of heroism or meritorious service performed between 6 December 1941 and 11 January 1944. Subsequent to the above period, personnel may apply for the medal if they possess a letter of commendation from the same higher authority providing the award is specifically mentioned.

Page 25, Items 47-51: Using the traditional sequence of "Senior Service First", these items should be listed in the order: 48, 49, 51, 50 and 47.

Page 27, Items 66 and 67: The award criteria for the two Occupation Medals are worth repeating since they rank highest on the list of items which many veterans forget to claim. The guidelines are the same for both, requiring a member of the Army, Navy, Marine Corps or Coast Guard to have served 30 consecutive days in any of the occupied territories after VE-Day and/or VJ-Day.

Page 26, Item 67: The Navy Occupation Medal was issued with two distinct reverse designs, one for Navy and Coast Guard recipients and one for the Marine Corps.

Page 28, Item 80: The Armed Forces Reserve Medal is issued with six reverse patterns; one each for the Army, Navy, Marine Corps, Air Force, Coast Guard and National Guard.

Page 30, Items 90a, 91a: The devices should be placed on the respective ribbons as follows:

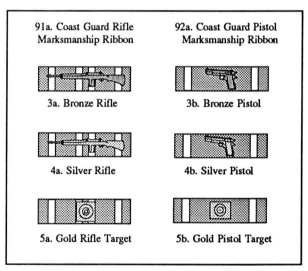

91a. Coast Guard Rifle Marksmanship Ribbon	92a. Coast Guard Pistol Marksmanship Ribbon
3a. Bronze Rifle	3b. Bronze Pistol
4a. Silver Rifle	4b. Silver Pistol
5a. Gold Rifle Target	5b. Gold Pistol Target

Page 33, Item 96: Some confusion seems to exist on the criteria for the Philippine Independence Ribbon/ Medal. The original standard ("...present for duty in the Philippines on 4 July 1946...") was modified in 1953 and, since that time, sentiment (and some very competent authorities) seem to favor the award to U.S. personnel who won either the Philippine Defense or Philippine Liberation Ribbons. However, U.S. military regulations require the receipt of **both** the Defense and Liberation Ribbons.

REQUEST PERTAINING TO MILITARY RECORDS

Please read instructions on the reverse. If more space is needed, use plain paper.

PRIVACY ACT OF 1974 COMPLIANCE INFORMATION. The following information is provided in accordance with 5 U.S.C. 552a(e)(3) and applies to this form. Authority for collection of the information is 44 U.S.C. 2907, 3101, and 3103, and E.O. 9397 of November 22, 1943. Disclosure of the information is voluntary. The principal purpose of the information is to assist the facility servicing the records in locating and verifying the correctness of the requested records or information to answer your inquiry. Routine uses of the information as established and published in accordance with 5 U.S.C.a(e)(4)(D) include the transfer of relevant information to appropriate Federal, State, local, or foreign agencies for use in civil, criminal, or regulatory investigations or prosecution. In addition, this form will be filed with the appropriate military records and may be transferred along with the record to another agency in accordance with the routine uses established by the agency which maintains the record. If the requested information is not provided, it may not be possible to service your inquiry.

SECTION I—INFORMATION NEEDED TO LOCATE RECORDS (Furnish as much as possible)

1. NAME USED DURING SERVICE (Last, first, and middle)	2. SOCIAL SECURITY NO.	3. DATE OF BIRTH	4. PLACE OF BIRTH

5. ACTIVE SERVICE, PAST AND PRESENT (For an effective records search, it is important that ALL service be shown below)

BRANCH OF SERVICE (Also, show last organization, if known)	DATES OF ACTIVE SERVICE DATE ENTERED	DATES OF ACTIVE SERVICE DATE RELEASED	Check one OFFICER	Check one ENLISTED	SERVICE NUMBER DURING THIS PERIOD

6. RESERVE SERVICE, PAST OR PRESENT   If "none," check here ▶ ☐

a. BRANCH OF SERVICE	b. DATES OF MEMBERSHIP FROM	b. DATES OF MEMBERSHIP TO	c. Check one OFFICER	c. Check one ENLISTED	d. SERVICE NUMBER DURING THIS PERIOD
			☐	☐	

7. NATIONAL GUARD MEMBERSHIP (Check one): ☐ a. ARMY ☐ b. AIR FORCE ☐ c. NONE

d. STATE	e. ORGANIZATION	f. DATES OF MEMBERSHIP FROM	f. DATES OF MEMBERSHIP TO	g. Check one OFFICER	g. Check one ENLISTED	h. SERVICE NUMBER DURING THIS PERIOD
				☐	☐	

8. IS SERVICE PERSON DECEASED ☐ YES ☐ NO   *If "yes," enter date of death.*

9. IS (WAS) INDIVIDUAL A MILITARY RETIREE OR FLEET RESERVIST ☐ YES ☐ NO

SECTION II—REQUEST

1. EXPLAIN WHAT INFORMATION OR DOCUMENTS YOU NEED; OR, CHECK ITEM 2; OR, COMPLETE ITEM 3 _____

2. IF YOU ONLY NEED A STATEMENT OF SERVICE check here ☐

3. LOST SEPARATION DOCUMENT REPLACEMENT REQUEST (Complete a or b, and c.)

☐ a. REPORT OF SEPARATION (DD Form 214 or equivalent)	YEAR ISSUED	This contains information normally needed to determine eligibility for benefits. It may be furnished only to the veteran, the surviving next of kin, or to a representative with veteran's signed release (item 5 of this form).
☐ b. DISCHARGE CERTIFICATE	YEAR ISSUED	This shows only the date and character at discharge. It is of little value in determining eligibility for benefits. It may be issued only to veterans discharged honorably or under honorable conditions; or, if deceased, to the surviving spouse.

c. EXPLAIN HOW SEPARATION DOCUMENT WAS LOST

4. EXPLAIN PURPOSE FOR WHICH INFORMATION OR DOCUMENTS ARE NEEDED

6. REQUESTER

a. IDENTIFICATION (check appropriate box)

☐ Same person identified in Section I   ☐ Surviving spouse

☐ Next of kin (relationship) _____

☐ Other (specify)

b. SIGNATURE (see instruction 3 on reverse side)   DATE OF REQUEST

5. RELEASE AUTHORIZATION, IF REQUIRED (Read instruction 3 on reverse side)

I hereby authorize release of the requested information/documents to the person indicated at right (item 7).

VETERAN SIGN HERE ▶ _____

(If signed by other than veteran show relationship to veteran.)

7. Please type or print clearly —   COMPLETE RETURN ADDRESS

Name, number and street, city, State and ZIP code _____

TELEPHONE NO. (include area code) ▶

180-106   NSN 7540-00-142-9360

STANDARD FORM 180 (Rev. 7-86)
Prescribed by NARA (36 CFR 1228.162(a))

15. BIBLIOGRAPHY

Abbott, P.E. and Tamplin, J.M.A.- *British Gallantry Awards*, 1971

Adjutant General of the Army- *American Decorations 1862-1926*, 1927

Belden, B.L.- *United States War Medals*, 1916

Committee on Veterans' Affairs, U.S. Senate- *Medal of Honor Recipients 1863-1978*, 1979

Dept. of Defense Manual DOD 1348.33M- *Manual of Military Decorations & Awards*, 1993

Dorling, H.T.- *Ribbons and Medals*, 1983

Gleim, A.F.- *United States Medals of Honor 1862-1989*, 1989

Gleim, A.F.- *War Department Gallantry Citations for Pre W W I Service*, 1986

Inter-American Defense Board- *Norms for Protocol, Symbols, Insignia and Gifts*, 1984

Kerrigan, E.- *American Badges and Insignia*, 1967

Kerrigan, E.- *American Medals and Decorations*, 1990

Kerrigan, E.- *American War Medals and Decorations*, 1971

Mayo, J.H.- *Medals and Decorations of the British Army & Navy*, 1897

McDowell, C.P.- *Military and Naval Decorations of the United States*, 1984

National Geographic Magazine, December, 1919

National Geographic Society- *Insignia and Decorations of the U.S. Armed Forces*, 1944

Strandberg, J.E. and Bender, R.J.- *The Call to Duty*, 1994

U.S. Air Force Instruction 36-2903- *Dress and Personal Appearance of U.S.A.F. Personnel*, 1994

U.S. Air Force Instruction 36-2803- *The Air Force Awards and Decorations Program*, 1994

U.S. Army Regulation 670-1- *Wear and Appearance of Army Uniforms and Insignia*, 1992

U.S. Army Regulation 672-5-1- *Military Awards*, 1989

U.S. Coast Guard Instruction M1020.6A- *U.S. Coast Guard Uniform Regulations*, 1985

U.S. Coast Guard Instruction M1650.25A- *Medals and Awards Manual*, 1992

U.S. Marine Corps Order P1020.34F- *U.S. Marine Corps Uniform Regulations*, 1995

U.S. Navy Instruction SECNAVINST 1650.1F- *Navy and Marine Corps Awards Manual*, 1991

U.S. Navy Instruction SECNAVINST 15665G- *United States Navy Uniform Regulations*, 1987

U.S. Navy Manual NAVPERS 15,790- *Decorations, Medals, Ribbons and Badges of the United States Navy, Marine Corps and Coast Guard, 1861-1948*, 1 July 1950

Vietnam Council on Foreign Relations- *Awards & Decorations of Vietnam*, 1972

Wilkins, P.A.- *The History of the Victoria Cross*, 1904

Wyllie, Col. R.E.- *Orders, Decorations and Insignia*, 1921

16. INDEX
NOTE: Numbers in Bold Italics Denote Illustrations

ORDER FORM

For additional copies of this book or other fine books by Medals of America Press, please use the order format below. Customer service is available Monday through Friday, 0900 hours to 1700 hours Eastern Standard Time.

"The Decorations of the Republic of Vietnam and Her Allies 1950 to 1975"
Beautifully colored guide to Republic of Vietnam Military and Civilian Decorations, medals, ribbons and unit awards. Also includes medals of the Vietnamese allies. *96 pages.*

Hardcover BK-10 . . . $24.95

"U.S. Military Medals 1939 to Present"
Complete and easy-to-use guide, U.S. Military Medals 1939 to Present is America's most detailed and complete book on US medals. Over 150 medals and ribbons in color. *80 pages.*

Hardcover BK 7 . . . $24.95
Softcover BK-6 . . . $19.95

"How to Claim Your or Your Family's Military Medals Free From the United States Government"
First published 20 years ago, over 20,000 veterans and their families have used this manual to claim their military awards. Updated every year, it furnishes background, instructions, forms and draft letters to claim personal awards or those of a family member as next of kin. *28 pages.*

Manual MP1 . . . $11.50 (includes postage)

"Complete Guide to Correct Ribbon Wear for the Army, Navy, Marines, Air Force and Coast Guard"
Booklet covers 1939 to present and has the complete order of precedence for every ribbon of the Army, Navy, Marines, Air Force and Coast Guard in full color and individually labeled. Facing pages show every ribbon device and its correct manner of wear for each service. *12 pages.*

Softcover PM-1 . . . $5.00

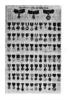

Full Color, Full Size United States Medal Chart
This chart covers WWII to the Gulf War and has each medal shown in its full size with a brief description under its name. Also includes the 12 most commonly awarded foreign medals. Printed on 100 lb. gloss enamel and varnished, this 25" x 38" chart can be framed.

MC1 . . . $10.50 (includes postage)

Medals of America Catalog
All U.S. Military Medals and badges, display cases, miniature medals and ribbons. America's largest source of U.S. Military Awards. Our catalog is a reference guide in itself. *32 pages.*

$2.00

TELEPHONE ORDERS: Call 1-803-862-6425 or 1-803-862-7494. Have your credit card ready.
FAX ORDERS: 1-803-862-7495.
POSTAL ORDERS: Medals of America Press, 1929 Fairview Road, Fountain Inn, SC 29644.

Company Name: _____

Name: _____

Address: _____

City _____ State: _____ Zip Code: _____

Sales Tax: Please add 5% for books shipped to South Carolina addresses.
Shipping: Book Rate $4.00 for the first book and $2.00 for each additional book. All books mailed First Class.
Air Mail: $3.50 per book in additional to regular mailing charge.

Payment:

☐ Check ☐ Credit Card: Visa, MasterCard, Discover

Card Number: __ __ __ __-__ __ __ __-__ __ __ __-__ __ __ __

Name on Card _____ Expiration Date: ___ / ___